BOOST YOUR SKILLS

in Computer Basics and Windows 11

Greg P. Marshall II

LABYRINTH
LEARNING®

Co-Founder:
Brian Favro

Product Manager:
Jason Favro

Learning Solutions Architect:
Laura Popelka

Production Manager:
Debra Grose

Senior Editor:
Alexandra Mummery

eLearning Specialist:
Lauren Carlson

Cover Design:
Sam Anderson Design

LABYRINTH

LEARNING ®

Boost Your Skills In Computer Basics and Windows 11
By Greg P. Marshall II

Copyright © 2024 by Labyrinth Learning

Labyrinth Learning
PO Box 2669
Danville, CA 94526
800.522.9746
On the web at: lablearning.com

Photo and illustration credits: p. 9, © afrank99 (own work) via Wikimedia Commons; © Aidan C. Siegel, Aido2002 via Wikimedia Commons; p. 145, © Darkone (own work) via Wikimedia Commons; p. 146, © Harke (own work) via Wikimedia Commons

Item:	1-64061-578-4
ISBN-13:	978-1-64061-578-6

Table of Contents

UNIT 2
File Management

Preface

Boost Your Skills in Computer Basics and Windows 11 provides new users with a solid foundation in computer basics, file management, and more. We begin Unit 1 with a discussion of the Microsoft Windows operating system, including signing on, controlling app windows, multitasking, creating a Microsoft account, using the online Office apps, and emailing. In Unit 2 we move on to discussing key file management best practices. And in Unit 3, we get on the Internet to do some web searching!

New to this edition: This text has been updated with new screen captures and steps to address updates to Windows 11, the online Office apps, OneDrive, and Edge.

About the Author

Greg P. Marshall II (BS, Information Technology Management) has been a computer user for most of his life. He enjoys sharing his skill and passion for the digital world with new users. With more than twenty years of experience, Greg teaches a wide variety of topics, from Microsoft Office to web design, digital cameras, search engine optimization (SEO), and new subjects as they emerge. Greg was the Director of Community Education at Whatcom Community College for fifteen years, where he wrote and developed new curricula for the computer and business programs. Currently, Greg is a freelance technologist and works with schools and businesses on their technology needs. He lectures regionally and nationally on future trends in computers and on workshop development. When he has some spare time, he enjoys digital photography, spending time with his son, and exploring the nation's back roads while traveling.

UNIT 1: WINDOWS BASICS

In this unit, you will start exploring Microsoft's operating system, known as Windows. Topics covered in Chapters 1–2 include starting and properly shutting down the computer, logging in, using a mouse, navigating the basic features of the opening screen known as the Desktop, employing touch controls, and switching between apps. Chapter 3 addresses how and why you should create a Microsoft account. Topics covered in Chapters 4 and 5 include how to work with apps, how and where to save your work, using the Word online app for typing and editing, how to use email, and email safety.

CHAPTER 1

Getting Your First Look

LEARNING OBJECTIVES

- Log in to the computer using a username and a password
- Describe the basic layout of the Windows Desktop screen
- Use the mouse to right-click and drag
- Work with the Start menu
- Shut down the computer correctly

Windows 11 is the newest version of Microsoft's operating system. With this release, Microsoft continues toward its goal of making access to the functionality of the computer easier and less frustrating for both new and experienced users. In this chapter, you will start the computer, navigate basic features of the opening screen known as the Desktop, use the mouse skills necessary to navigate in Windows, and properly shut down the computer.

Learning Resources: **boostyourskills.lablearning.com**

📂 Case Study: Starting Something New

Cherize moved into her son's home. Her son, Patrick, wanted Cherize to have access to the family computer so she could play games such as Solitaire, learn to use email, and search the Internet. To give Cherize privacy, her son set up a separate username and password.

Cherize was scared the first time she sat down at the computer, but Patrick said, "Push the Power button and start using it. And don't worry; you won't break anything." Her son explained the login screen to her and showed her how to enter her password.

When another colorful screen appeared, Patrick said, "That's the Desktop. Here is the Start button that gives you access to all of your programs. Single-click the icons in the Start menu to see the programs you have."

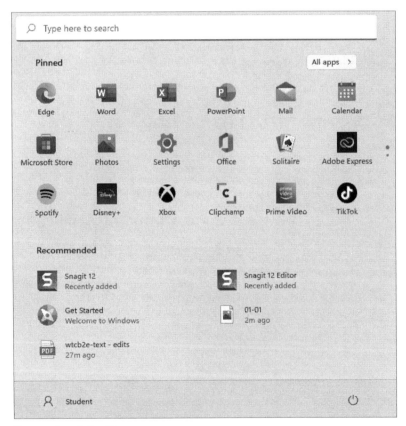

Example of the Start menu screen

At first she had difficulty, but after a while, Cherize became more comfortable with the mouse and rarely had to look at it before clicking. She began to think, "Using this computer is going to be fun."

Logging In to Windows

Most computer systems used in schools and businesses are **networked**, or connected. An important part of keeping a network secure is making sure everyone using computers on the network is authorized to do so. Logging in to the computer is the process of entering your username and password to gain access to the computer and network.

Passwords

A critical piece of the login process is the password. Your password allows you into the computer. Your password must be entered correctly every time. For example, *Pa!z4EV* is not the same as *pa!z4ev*.

Warning! Passwords should never be shared. Sharing passwords is one of the top reasons people have their computer and financial information stolen.

Creating Your Own Passwords

When creating your own password for a home or office computer, don't use familiar names, birthdays, or common words that can be easily guessed. A secure password will contain a mixture of uppercase and lowercase letters, numbers, and punctuation.

The following are some examples of good and poor passwords:

EXAMPLES OF PASSWORDS	
Good Passwords	**Poor Passwords**
!GreeN2	Fido
8Ate8	Johndoe
Fun2Dr1v	12345678
AcEsn8s	Password

Password Managers

Password managers manage all your passwords and work across all your devices, including your phone, computers, and tablets. When you visit a website that requires you to log in, the password manager will automatically fill your password in. The only password you have to remember is the one for the password manager!

Some of the most popular password managers include 1Password, LastPass, RoboForm, Avira, and Enpass.

What Happens During the Startup Process?

From the moment you turn on the computer and throughout the login process, the computer and Windows are working together to get ready for you. Windows is not one giant program but rather a collection of hundreds of little programs, so as the computer starts, the various parts and pieces of Windows are starting as well. Together they form the **operating system** that we see and work with on the screen.

HANDS-ON 1.1 Log In to Windows

In this exercise, you will log in to your computer.

1. If necessary, turn on the computer and monitor.

After a pause, the computer begins starting up, which usually takes about a minute. When the startup process is complete, the lock screen appears.

2. Click the **lock** screen to bring up the sign-in screen.

The lock screen covers the sign-in screen with a changing image and provides the date and time. If you take too long when entering your login and password, the lock screen will reappear.

3. Click the appropriate login from the lower-left corner of the screen. If you are the only person who uses your computer, your login may be the only one listed.

Notice that clicking on a login causes it to show in the middle of the screen. In the following example we have chosen Student Marshall, but you should use your login:

4. Enter your password into the blank password line and click the **arrow** button. This will take you to the Desktop.

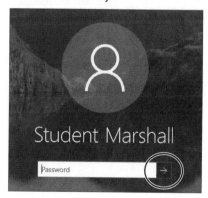

The Windows Desktop

Once you have logged in to the computer, you will be looking at the Windows Desktop. The Desktop is the primary work area in Windows, and like your desk at school, all the apps you are working with are placed on the Desktop.

The Desktop has many unique features that help you to be more efficient when using the computer.

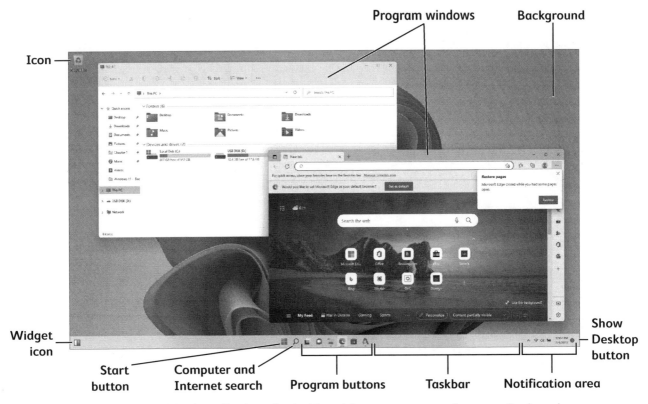

This is what the Windows Desktop looks like with some common features displayed.

BEHIND THE SCREEN

Basic Computer Components

Your computer is a collection of hardware parts working together with Windows and other software applications. Knowing the name and function of various components can give you a better understanding of the computing process.

Processor

The processor is often referred to as the "brain" of the computer. The central processing unit (CPU) does all the processing that keeps programs running, moves the cards when you play Solitaire, and does the math in your spreadsheet programs.

How quickly these processes are carried out is largely determined by the gigahertz (GHz) rating of the CPU. A larger GHz rating means the processor is capable of significantly more (billions more!) processing cycles per second.

Intel's i9 is a popular processor for computers running Windows.

Hard Drive

The **hard drive** is the **permanent storage** device in the computer. You can think of the hard drive as a large filing cabinet where all the files and programs that run on the computer are stored.

Traditional hard drives use spinning magnetic platters to store information on. These drives are inexpensive to make and are capable of storing huge amounts of data.

A traditional hard drive from Western Digital

An SSD from Crucial

A NAND SSD from Samsung

Newer hard drives are solid state. These hard drives contain no moving parts and are much quicker in loading data and programs. They are referred to as SSDs (solid-state drives). The newest SSDs are very small and look more like RAM than a traditional hard drive. They are generally referred to as a NAND SSD.

Random Access Memory (RAM)

Hard drives operate at a relatively slow speed, so your computer does not run programs directly from the hard drive. When a program is used, it is first loaded into random access memory (RAM) to take advantage of the very high speed at which it allows data to be accessed by the CPU. As you edit a letter or make a drawing, the information is being stored in RAM. RAM is considered temporary memory, though, because unlike the hard drive, when the computer is turned off, all of the data in RAM is lost.

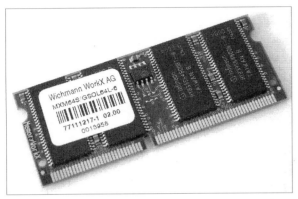

An example of random access memory for a laptop

Universal Serial Bus (USB)

A universal serial bus (USB) port is a small rectangular port or connector now common on all computers that allows you to connect various pieces of equipment to your computer using a single standardized cord and plug. USB ports come in three basic sizes that all provide the same connection services. Once a device is connected via a USB port, Windows will recognize the equipment and help with its configuration. Before USB, different equipment had special connectors and cables, and it was much more difficult for new users to set up their computers.

A cable you can plug into a USB device

A typical USB port located on the front or side of a computer

Here are examples of a USB plug and port. Notice the universal symbol for USB on both the plug and equipment.

Secure Digital (SD) Card

An SD card is a type of storage device typically found on digital cameras and other portable devices. Many desktop and laptop computers now come with an SD card reader to make accessing data from devices easier. Some devices use micro SD cards, which are about the size of your thumbnail!

This is an example of an SD card from SanDisk.

This micro SD card has an adapter, which allows you to use the card in a standard SD card drive.

Start Button

The square button in the center area at the bottom of the screen that displays the Windows logo is called the Start button. Access to most of Windows' features, your software, and your documents starts from this button in what's called the Start menu. Microsoft wants you to remember that everything "starts" with this little square button.

Icons

Icons are small pictures on the screen that represent programs or other features. You can launch these programs and features by double-clicking on their icons. On the desktop, you will notice an icon in the upper-left corner labeled Recycle Bin. This represents the Recycle Bin folder, where files are moved when deleted (as discussed later in this book).

Typical Windows icons

Notification Area

The notification area is located on the taskbar in the lower-right corner of the computer screen. The notification area contains icons for programs that are currently running but don't necessarily need a lot of user interaction, such as antivirus programs, Internet connection software, Microsoft Outlook email, and possibly the software that allows your computer to communicate with your printer.

Tip! If you use your mouse pointer to hover over an icon in the notification area, a small ScreenTip will appear that tells you what that program does or is doing. ScreenTips are helpful if you're curious about what's going on in your computer.

Network Connection

Most computers will be connected to the Internet and, in a school or business environment, to a local network. This connection can be made either by using a network cable that plugs into the network port on your computer or by using the radio transmitter in your computer to connect wirelessly. This is known as *WI-Fi*.

Besides providing you access to the Internet, the network connection at school or work may also give you access to printers and shared documents.

Using a Mouse

The mouse is your main tool for controlling programs on the Windows Desktop. Moving the mouse with your hand controls the movements of the **mouse pointer** on the screen. With your mouse on a flat surface (a table or mouse pad), place your hand on the mouse as shown below so your index finger rests lightly on or above the left mouse button. You may find that dragging your thumb on the flat surface next to the mouse as you move and click can help you control the movement of the mouse.

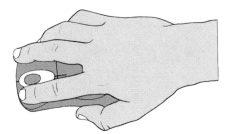

When you hold the mouse, your index finger should rest lightly on the left button.

Note! Keep your wrist straight when using the mouse. The top of the mouse should point toward the top of the mouse pad or workspace. Don't steer the mouse like a car, as twisting/turning it disorients the mouse pointer.

Mouse Motions

There are five basic actions that you can take with the mouse: point, click, drag, double-click, and right-click. With an understanding of these basic actions, you can use the mouse to control most features in Windows.

MOUSE MOTIONS	
Motion	**Notes and How to Do It**
Point	▪ Used to view ScreenTips or highlight icons and buttons before selecting. ▪ Hold the tip of the mouse pointer over an element on the screen. ▪ Keep the mouse steady. ▪ Only the tip of the mouse pointer is active.
Click (single-click)	▪ Used to "push" an onscreen button. ▪ Point to an onscreen element and push the left mouse button one time. ▪ Hold the mouse still and click gently.
Drag	▪ Used to move items around the screen, select text, and perform other tasks/commands. ▪ Similar to a click, but do not let go of the mouse button. ▪ Point to an onscreen element, click and hold down the left mouse button, and move the mouse until the onscreen element is in the desired location. This action is often referred to as *drag and drop*.
Double-click	▪ Used to start a program or open a file/folder. ▪ Point to an onscreen element and quickly click the left mouse button twice. ▪ Hold the mouse still and click gently. ▪ Be patient! A double-click doesn't have to be lightning fast, as you have about a second to complete the two clicks. Slowing down your clicking speed will help keep you from wiggling the mouse.
Right-click	▪ Used to display a pop-up menu of options that relate to the object. ▪ Point to an onscreen element and click the right mouse button once. ▪ Dismiss a pop-up menu by (left) clicking another place on the screen or tapping Esc on the keyboard.

⌐ HANDS-ON 1.2 Use the Mouse

In this exercise, you will use the mouse to point at, click on, and drag the Recycle Bin around the Desktop.

1. Follow these steps to start using the mouse:

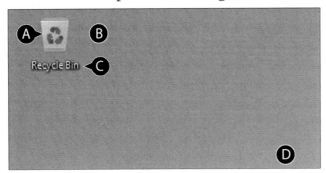

Ⓐ Point with the mouse over the Recycle Bin.

Ⓑ Point away from the Recycle Bin.

Ⓒ Click (tap and release) with the left mouse button on the **Recycle Bin** icon.

Ⓓ Point away from the Recycle Bin (don't click) and notice that the icon stays selected (highlighted).

2. Follow these steps to drag the Recycle Bin to a new location on the Desktop:

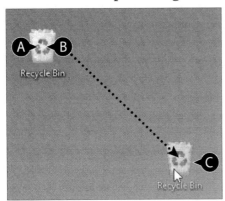

Ⓐ Point at the Recycle Bin.

Ⓑ Press the left mouse button, and while keeping it depressed, move the mouse to drag the Recycle Bin to the right.

Ⓒ Release the mouse button at a new destination of your choice.

3. Drag the Recycle Bin back to its original location on the Desktop.

This course is supported with online resources, simulations, and more. When you see the cloud icon, go to the online resources at: boostyourskills.lablearning.com

For more practice using the mouse, click the "Get Some Mousercise" link in the Chapter 1 section in the online resources.

Passwords and Account Settings

All Windows users have their own login and password that allow them to connect to their various personal settings for the computer, as well as to other online accounts they may have that are connected to Windows.

Accessing Account Settings

The circular "person" icon of the individual logged in to the computer is located on the bottom of the Start menu. This user's name and their circular "person" icon, which together we will call the user icon/name button, gives you the option to change account settings when clicked. Here you can access and change the various options related to your login account, such as your login information, password, your user account picture, and options for syncing your computer with other devices.

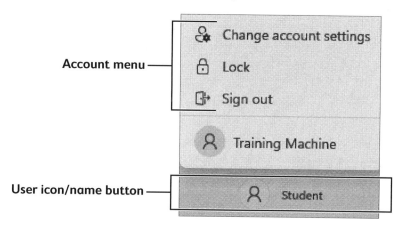

- **Sign-In Options:** From this screen you can change your password and set whether you need to enter your password again when you use your computer after it has been in **sleep mode**.
- **Access Work or School:** At work or school, you may be allowed to connect your personal computer to the network. If this is an option, you will be given specific instructions for how to do so.
- **Other Users:** On a home computer, and if you have administrator privileges, you can add other users to the computer. The Create One for a Child button allows you

to create accounts for children that have time limits on use and only allow visits to safe websites.

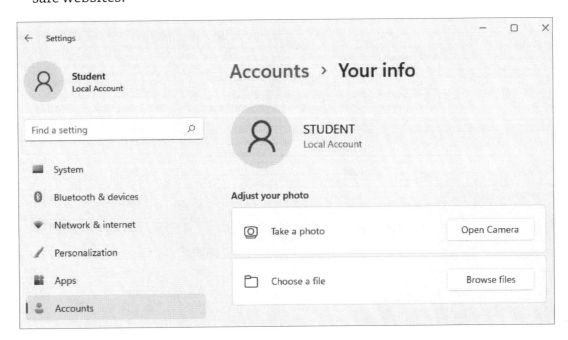

Warning! Never rely just on software to protect your kids online. Be proactive and teach them how to protect themselves.

Signing Out and Switching Users

Signing out of the computer is different from turning off the computer. Before signing out, you need to save your files to the hard drive. This is because when you do sign out, the computer closes the programs you were using and removes your login information and settings from memory so it will be ready for a new user to log on.

Note! Signing out does not shut off power to the computer; the computer is left running, and it is ready for another user to log in.

Switch Users

Multiple users can be signed on to a single computer at the same time, and each user can customize the visual environment of the computer to meet his or her needs. Unlike when you sign out, when you simply switch users, the previous user's information, screen settings, and programs are set aside in the computer's RAM, and the new user's information is employed, but the previous user's information can be quickly reimplemented if that person signs back in because it is saved in the RAM.

The ability to switch users is most helpful in a home environment in which more than one person shares a computer.

Locking the Computer

Locking the computer protects your PC from unauthorized use when you leave your desk. Locking causes the lock screen to display. To see your screen and continue working, you must re-enter your password.

LOGGING OFF AND SWITCHING USERS	
Task	**Procedure**
Log off Windows	Click the Start button. Click your user icon/name button at the top of the menu and then click Sign Out.
Switch users	Click the Start button. Click your user icon/name button and then choose the desired user from the list.
Lock/Unlock Windows	Click your user icon/name button and choose Lock. This will lock the computer and show the lock screen. To unlock the computer, click the lock screen and then enter your password on the sign-in screen when it appears.

HANDS-ON 1.3 Lock the Computer

In this exercise, you will give the lock command and then log back in using your own username and password.

1. Click the **Start** button.

2. Follow these steps to lock the computer:

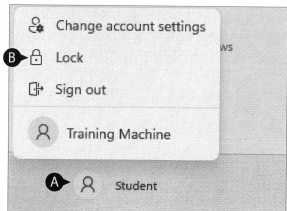

Ⓐ Click the **user icon/name** button.

Ⓑ Choose **Lock** from the menu.

There will be a pause as Windows prepares to display the lock screen. Wait for this screen to appear before continuing with the next step.

3. Click the **lock** screen.

4. Type your password in the password box and then tap ⌷Enter⌷ on the keyboard.
   After a pause, Windows returns you to the Desktop. You could just as easily have logged in as someone else by choosing their name from the corner of the login screen and entering their password.

The Start Menu

The Start menu is the one place you can go to launch most of the programs installed on your computer. Like all menus, the Start menu is a collection of **commands**, and these particular ones allow you to launch all of the programs that come with Windows. Commands on a menu often have a descriptive label and an icon. When you install a new program, Windows adds a command for it to the Start menu.

Commands

A command is a link that can launch (start or open) a file, folder, or app, or that can execute a variety of other tasks. You might compare a command to a light switch on a wall used to turn on a ceiling light; clicking (or double-clicking) a command launches the object to which it is linked. More than one command can be linked to the same object. Commands can be located on the Desktop, in a menu, on a toolbar, or on a Ribbon.

HANDS-ON 1.4 Display and Dismiss the Start Menu

In this exercise, you will display and dismiss the Start menu using both the mouse and the keyboard.

1. Click the **Start** ▦ button to display the Start menu.
   Note the upper and lower panes of the Start menu.

2. Click the **Start** button again to dismiss the Start menu.

3. Press the **Windows** ⊞ key on the keyboard to display the Start menu.

4. Press the **Windows** key again to dismiss the Start menu.
   It's easy to dismiss the Start menu if you pull it up by mistake.

The Start Menu Panes

The Start menu is divided into panes:

- The top pane shows a list of all pinned apps. You can add frequently used apps by pinning them to the Start menu.
- The bottom pane lists recommended documents and apps. These are items you have recently used.

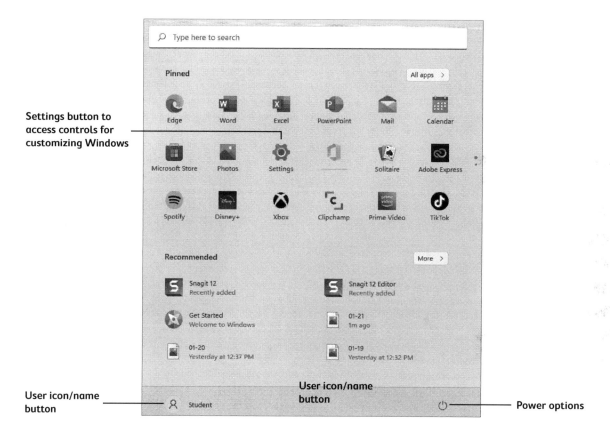

Tip! The appearance of the Start menu may vary depending on your version of Windows, but all Start menus function in the same manner.

You will notice that the terms app and program are used interchangeably. There is no longer a big difference between the two words, and both terms are used to describe a set of instructions that tell the computer or device to perform a specific task.

HANDS-ON 1.5 Launch a Program from the Start Menu

In this exercise, you will launch the Calculator app from the Start menu.

1. Click the **Start** button and then click the **All Apps** button.

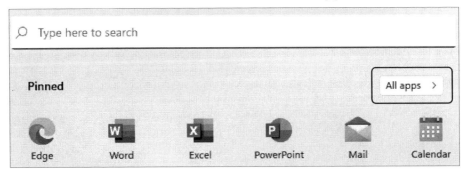

2. Choose **Calculator**.

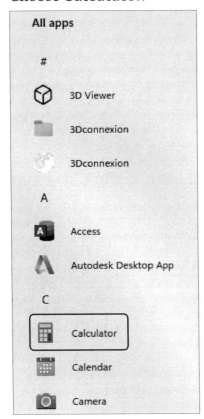

The Start menu collapses and the Calculator app opens.

3. Close the Calculator app by clicking the **Close** button (the "X") in the upper-right corner.

. . . .

The Pinned and Recommended Lists

Windows 11 automatically adds commands for apps to the Pinned list in the Start menu. Sometimes an app is added to the list the first time you launch it. Other times you may need to use a program twice to have it added to the list. When the Pinned apps list becomes full, the command for the app that has been unused the longest is removed. You can also add and delete apps to suit your needs. The Recommended section of the Start menu shows the documents and files you have opened most recently.

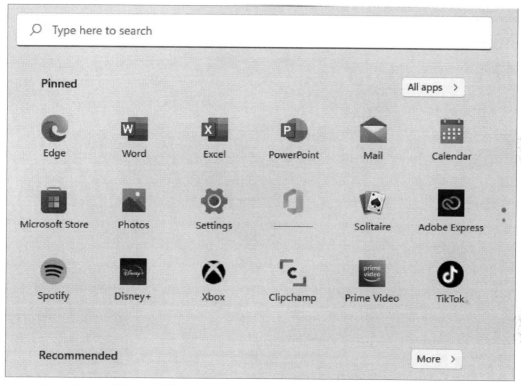

Your Pinned list will look different from this example, as it will show the apps you have used. The Recommended list changes often.

Pinning Commands to the Start Menu

Commands for any app can be easily **pinned** to the Start menu. You pin a command to the Start menu to make it easier to access.

Moving Apps on the Start Menu

You can move apps around on the Start menu as you like, and you can move an app straight to the top of the menu by right-clicking the app icon with the mouse to open a menu of commands. If you have many apps, there may be more than one screen that you can scroll through on the Start menu.

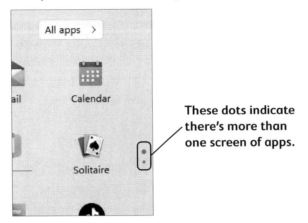

These dots indicate there's more than one screen of apps.

HANDS-ON 1.6 Customize the Start Menu

In this exercise you will add and position an app on the Start menu.

1. Click the **Start** menu, click the **All Apps** button, and find the Calculator app (but don't click it yet).

2. Right-click the **Calculator** icon and choose **Pin to Start**.

3. Click the (< Back) button.
   Notice that the Calculator icon appears at the bottom of the Pinned section. If you can't see the Calculator icon, use the down arrow on the keyboard to scroll down through the Pinned section.

4. Right-click the **Calculator** icon in the Pinned section and choose **Move to Front**.
   The Calculator icon is now the first icon on the Pinned menu.

5. Click and hold the **Calculator** icon and drag it to a new location on the Pinned menu.

Adding Folders to the Start Menu

You can add folders to the Start menu to organize icons and shortcuts. When you drag one icon onto another icon on the Start menu, this triggers the creation of a folder. More icons can then be added to the folder by dragging and dropping icons onto the folder.

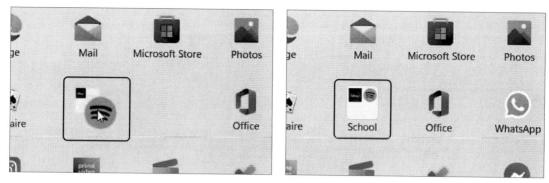

You can start the programs in the folder by clicking to open the folder and then clicking the desired icon.

Start menu folders can be renamed to help with the organization of apps and shortcuts. For example, you could create a folder for all your social media apps, another one for games, and another folder for those apps you use for school.

Note! Does this seem a little familiar? It might. It's the same way folders are created on your phone or tablet.

HANDS-ON 1.7 Customize the Start Menu

In this exercise, you will add a folder to the Start menu and set a custom name for it.

1. Click the **Start** button.

2. On the Start menu, click and drag the icon of your choice onto another icon and then release your mouse button.
   Notice how a folder is created with both icons in it.

3. Click the folder you created and then the default title; type: **School**

4. Tap ⎡Enter⎤ to complete the name change.

5. Click outside the Start menu to close both the menu and the folder.

6. Click the **Start** button and verify that the folder has been renamed.
   Leave the folder open for the next exercise.

Deleting a Start Menu Folder

Deleting a menu folder is easy. The selected folder is deleted once there is only one icon or shortcut left in the folder. At this point the last icon or shortcut is placed back on the Start menu and the folder is automatically deleted.

HANDS-ON 1.8 Delete a Folder

In this exercise, you will remove one of the icons from the folder you created to automatically delete the folder.

1. Click the **Start** button to open the Start menu and then click your **School** folder.

2. Drag one of the icons out of the folder back into the Start menu.
   The folder is automatically deleted, and the remaining icon is moved back to the Start menu.

Shutting Down

Windows is a very large collection of programs. If it is not shut down properly, you may discover upon restarting your computer that error messages appear—or even worse, that Windows won't start at all. This is because Windows needs time to properly shut down all of its software parts and pieces correctly, and just turning off the power doesn't allow enough time to do this.

Shut-Down Methods

There are three ways to shut down Windows, depending on what you want to do next. The following available options are displayed via the Start button using the Power button and the Power button menu: Sleep, Shut Down, and Restart.

Self-Assessment

To check your knowledge of the key concepts introduced in this chapter, complete this Self-Assessment quiz.

1. Access to most features in Windows 11 is through the Start button located in the center area at the bottom of the screen. **true false**

2. Icons are small pictures that represent programs or other features. **true false**

3. Sleep mode is used to save energy when the computer is not going to be operated for a while. **true false**

4. Drag and drop is used to move icons on the screen. **true false**

5. It's okay to simply switch the power off when you're done using the computer. **true false**

6. It is best for everyone to share one login and password on a computer. **true false**

7. Which of these is the best password?

   A. Fido

   B. G476rty

   C. JohnSmith

   D. Password

8. Which of these is NOT a mouse action?

   A. Single-click

   B. Double-click

   C. Skip

   D. Point

9. Which item is NOT on the Power menu?

   A. Sleep

   B. Restart

   C. Shut Down

   D. Power System

10. Icons _____.

   A. are small images that can represent documents, photos, and apps

   B. can be found in many areas of Windows, including the Desktop and the taskbar

   C. act as the start buttons for programs

   D. All of the above

Skill Builders

....

SKILL BUILDER 1.1 Organize the Start Menu

In this exercise, you will add app icons to the Start menu and organize the menu.

1. Click the **Start** button and click **All Apps**.

2. Right-click the **Clock** app and choose **Pin to Start**.

3. Right-click the **Windows Media Player Legacy** app and choose **Pin to Start**.

4. Right-click the **Clock** app on the Pinned list and choose **Move to Front**. Do the same with the **Windows Media Player Legacy** app.

5. Move the **Clock** icon from the top Pinned row to the start of the second row.

6. Right-click the **Windows Media Player Legacy** app and choose **Unpin from Start**.

7. Right-click the **Clock** app and choose **Unpin from Start**.

....

SKILL BUILDER 1.2 Switch Users

In this exercise, you will switch from one user login to another.

Before You Begin: Skip this exercise if there is only one user listed on the Windows login screen. You need at least two user accounts to switch between users.

1. Click the **Start** button.

2. Follow these steps to switch users:

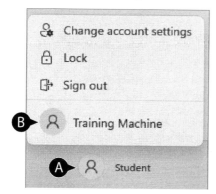

   Ⓐ Click the **user icon/name** button.

   The user icon/name button will feature a generic user icon picture or an actual image if the user has included a picture in their account settings.

   Ⓑ Choose a different user from the list of users.

   After a pause, Windows displays the lock screen.

3. Type your password and then tap Enter.

   Windows will now make the switch. This can take 15 seconds or more to accomplish, depending on the speed of your computer and the amount of RAM available for the operation.

4. Switch back to your account by clicking the **user icon/name** button and choosing your login.

   If you have not yet verified your account with Microsoft, at this point you may get a message that walks you through the process of verification.

5. Type your password and then tap Enter.

   There will be another pause as Windows switches you back to your Desktop. Notice that everything is just how you left it before switching to the other username.

SKILL BUILDER 1.3 Change Your Password

In this exercise, you will change your login password. This is the procedure to use on your home computer, not on school or public computers.

Before You Begin: Keep in mind that you are changing the password to your online Microsoft Live account associated with this login. Write down your new password and keep it in a safe location.

1. Click your **user icon/name** button at the bottom of the Start menu and then choose **Change Account Settings** from the menu that appears.

2. Choose **Accounts→Sign-In Options** from the menu.

3. Click **Password** to expand the menu and then click the **Change** button.
   After a moment, a new web browser window will appear.

4. Enter your current password and click **Sign In**.

5. From the Password block, click **Change Password**.

6. Enter your current password (again) in the space marked *Old Password*.

7. Enter your new password in the space marked *Create New Password* and repeat in the space marked *Confirm New Password*.
   You are changing your password. Write down your new password so you don't forget it! You will need it the next time you sign in.

8. Click the **Submit** button to complete the procedure.

9. Close the web browser window.

SKILL BUILDER 1.4 Shut Down

In this exercise, you will shut down the computer properly.

1. Make sure that all of your open apps are closed.

2. From the Start menu choose **Power→Shut Down**.
   The computer will take a minute or two to complete its shutdown tasks. Be patient!

3. If the computer doesn't turn off the power automatically, you will need to manually power off the computer and the monitor.

Warning! Sometimes Windows will hang up when closing and will stop responding. It is best to give the computer a few minutes to correct the problem before turning the power off manually and overriding Windows.

CHAPTER 2

Starting and Controlling Apps

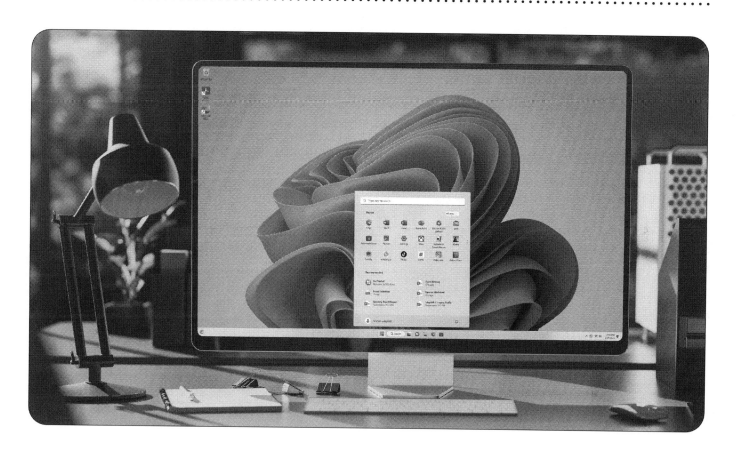

LEARNING OBJECTIVES

- Minimize, maximize, resize, and move app windows

- Use touch controls

- Describe the basic features of the Windows 11 taskbar

- Multitask effectively using the taskbar

- Access commands using the notification area

- Use the Action Center

Although apps (programs) from many different software companies are installed on your computer, the Windows operating system provides standardized tools for launching and controlling apps. In this chapter, you will become familiar with controlling an app window, using touch controls, working with the taskbar, and beginning to multitask by opening and switching between multiple programs.

Learning Resources: **boostyourskills.lablearning.com**

📂 Case Study: Starting at the Beginning

William is going back to school and has bought a new computer to help him complete his homework. He has very little experience using a computer and feels a bit confused by all of the programs. He has tried clicking on the Desktop icons and has clicked on the Start menu, but the apps have so many different purposes: Several play music, one is like a checkbook, one is for drawing pictures, another is a notepad, and there also are card games. Before learning the different applications he will be using to do his homework, he decides to first learn what the programs have in common. If he can learn the standardized Windows features used in most programs, it will be much easier to learn new apps. William starts by learning how to control the programs he has opened.

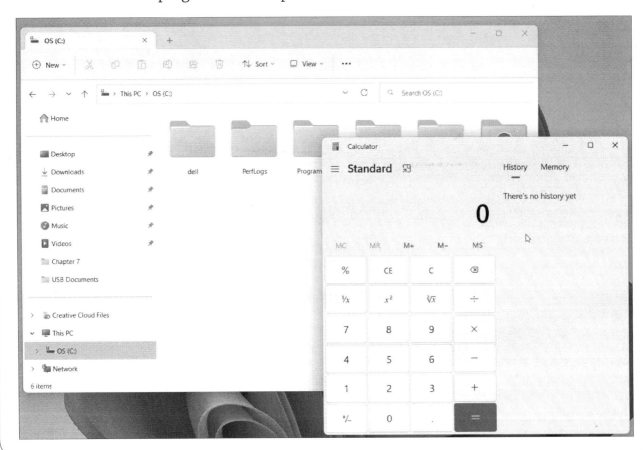

Controlling App Windows

Every app you open is displayed within its own window. This window, known as the app window, has controls and features that are similar in most programs. These basic controls are Windows standards; learn to use them in one app, and you will be able to work with similar controls in most new programs you use.

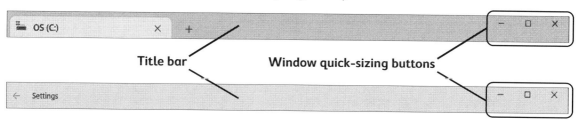

Here is an example of an app window for two different apps that come with Windows. The quick-sizing buttons and title bar are standard controls in all app windows.

Quick-Sizing Buttons

Quick-sizing buttons are used to reconfigure or close an app window. All apps use the same four quick-sizing buttons: Minimize, Maximize, Restore Down, and Close.

WINDOW QUICK-SIZING BUTTONS		
Button	**Name**	**How It Works**
−	Minimize	Removes the app window from the screen but continues to run it and leaves its app button on the taskbar
□	Maximize	Enlarges an app window to fill the screen
❐	Restore Down	Resizes an app window to the smaller size it was before it was last maximized
×	Close	Exits an app
📁	App button (on taskbar)	Represents open apps (each has an image representing the app that is open)/minimizes an open window or reopens a window that has been minimized

The Minimize and Maximize Buttons

The Minimize button shrinks the app window from the Desktop, leaving only its app button on the taskbar. The app continues to run. To open the app window again to the size it was before it was minimized, click the app's button on the taskbar.

Tip! If an app window is open, you also can click its app button on the taskbar to minimize the window.

The Maximize button does just the opposite of the Minimize button. Maximize enlarges an app to fill the entire Desktop so that other programs become hidden behind it.

Why minimize or maximize programs? Having multiple programs open on your Desktop can be like having a messy desk. Minimizing windows will hide the distracting clutter of open windows, while maximizing a window will simply cover other opened windows.

Minimizing Versus Closing

The Minimize button makes an app window shrink from the screen, but it does not close the app. If you are in the middle of using Paint 3D and choose to minimize, the Paint 3D app button remains on the taskbar. When you click the app's taskbar button, the app will return to its previous size and be ready for you to use it.

When you click the Close button, you end your usage of Paint 3D and exit the app, and the app button is removed from the taskbar.

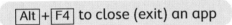

Alt + F4 to close (exit) an app

Tip! A quick way to close a minimized app is to right-click the app button on the taskbar. This displays the control menu (shown in the figure), which includes a Close Window command at the bottom.

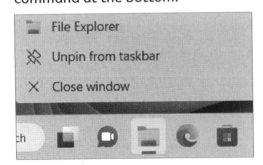

The Maximize and Restore Down Buttons

The center quick-sizing button toggles between the Maximize and Restore Down buttons depending on the state of the window; they are never shown at the same time. If you click Maximize, the center button changes to Restore Down. Conversely, if you click Restore Down, the center button changes to Maximize.

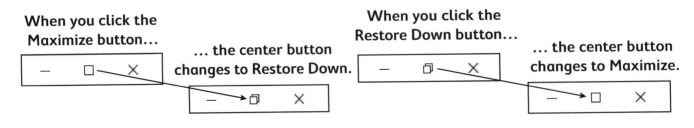

The App Button on the Taskbar

When an app is opened, its app button appears on the taskbar and displays the app's icon without a label. If you position the mouse cursor over the app button (without clicking), additional information about the app will be displayed in a ScreenTip. Clicking the app button allows you to minimize an open app window, restore a minimized window, or make an inactive app **active**.

 HANDS-ON 2.1 Use Quick-Sizing Buttons

In this exercise, you will open the File Explorer and use the quick-sizing buttons to maximize, restore down, and minimize the app window.

1. Click the **File Explorer** ⬚ button on the taskbar.
   The File Explorer app will open either maximized or in a restored-down size.

2. If the app window does not fill the screen, click the **Maximize** button.
   The app window enlarges to fill the entire Desktop (except for the taskbar). Also notice that the center quick-sizing button has changed to a Restore Down button.

Tip! It's usually a good idea to maximize any app window when it first opens to take full advantage of the entire screen.

3. Click the **Restore Down** button.
   Notice how the app window is restored back to its original, smaller size.

4. Click the **Minimize** button.

5. Click the **File Explorer** app button on the taskbar to restore the File Explorer program onto your Desktop.

Buttons on the taskbar help you identify the apps they are associated with. File Explorer, for example, uses a folder as its icon on the taskbar.

6. Click the **Close** button to exit File Explorer.

Menu Button

Some apps have a menu button located on the top-left corner of the app, just below the title bar.

This button is generally used instead of a menu bar across the top of the app, and it contains commands and settings for the app.

Tip! Sometimes the menu button is referred to as the "hamburger button" because it looks a bit like a hamburger!

Moving and Resizing App Windows

App windows can be moved around on the Desktop the way you move papers and objects around your desk at home. Unlike your desk at home, though, app windows can be resized to fill the Desktop or reduced to a smaller size.

Title Bar

The title bar at the top of every app window serves several purposes. It displays the name of the app, and it also may display the name of the document or other object being edited by that app. Control buttons are located at the right and left ends of the bar.

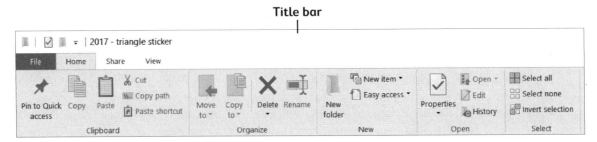

Finally, the title bar provides a handle that can be used to move the app window. If you position the tip of your mouse pointer over any empty space on the title bar (not its border), you can hold down your left mouse button and drag an app window around the Desktop.

Resizing a Window

An app window has a narrow border surrounding it. You can resize a window by dragging the border from any side or any corner. Dragging a side border will resize only that side of the window. Dragging a corner will resize both sides attached to the corner.

If your mouse pointer will not change to a double-headed arrow when you point at a border, then the app window cannot be resized.

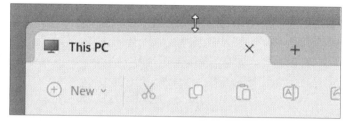

Some users find that resizing an app window is easier if they use the double-headed arrows that appear in the corner of the app window. They allow you to resize the app window in two directions at once.

The Snap Feature

Using the Snap feature is another way to maximize, restore down, or view two windows side by side on the Desktop. Snapping is accomplished by simply dragging windows to the top or sides of the Desktop.

Nonstandard App Windows

Although Windows establishes standards used by most programs, there are times when the standards are ignored or modified for appearance reasons or because certain functions are not necessary to use an app. In some programs the features are simply missing, while in other programs the features have a modified appearance or are grayed out and do not work.

RESIZING WINDOWS USING SNAP	
Task	Procedure
Maximize a window	▪ Click the title bar of a restored-down window and drag to the top edge of the Desktop until the mouse pointer touches it.
Restore down a window	▪ Click the title bar and drag a maximized window away from the top edge of the Desktop.
Display two windows side by side	▪ To make the window fill the left half of the Desktop, click the title bar and drag one window left until the mouse pointer touches the left edge of the Desktop. ▪ To make the window fill the right half of the Desktop, click the title bar and drag another window right until the mouse pointer touches the right edge of the Desktop.

HANDS-ON 2.2 Move, Resize, and Snap a Window

In this exercise, you will move, resize, and snap the File Explorer app window.

1. Click the **File Explorer** 📁 button on the taskbar.

2. If necessary, restore down the app window.

3. Click the title bar and drag the app window around the desktop.
   An app window cannot be resized using the mouse if it is maximized.

4. Practice resizing the app window using the borders or corners.

5. Initiate the Snap feature by using the title bar to drag the window to the left edge of the Desktop until the mouse pointer touches the edge.

6. Repeat step 5 by dragging the window to the right edge, the top edge, and finally away from all edges.

7. Click the **Close** button to exit File Explorer.

Touch Controls

The more recent versions of Windows support the use of touch **gestures** on computers and devices that have touchscreens, like tablets and smartphones. Using touch, you can move and control objects on the screen using one, two, or three fingers. If you have a precision touchpad on your laptop, you will be able to use these advanced controls.

HANDS-ON 2.3 Determine If You Have a Touchscreen

In this exercise, you will check to see if your Windows computer has a touchscreen.

1. Click **Start** and select the **Settings** icon.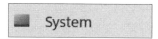

2. From Settings, click the **System** icon.

   System

3. On the Systems page, scroll down and click **About**. On the right side of the screen, look for the text *Pen and touch*. The text to the right will tell you whether your computer supports touch gestures.

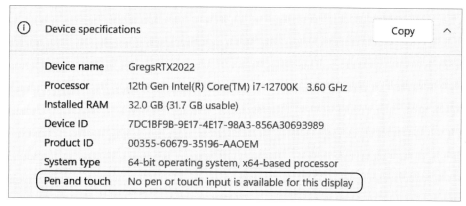

This computer does not support touch gestures.

4. Close the window.

. . . .

Touch Gestures

Touch gestures that involve moving a finger across the screen of your laptop or device while your finger is lightly touching the screen give the computer commands. The following are some examples:

USING TOUCH GESTURES		
Task	**Procedure**	
Open the Action Center	▪ Swipe in from the right edge of the screen.	
Open Task view	▪ Swipe in from the left edge of the screen.	
View the title bar	▪ Swipe down from the top of the screen. This allows you to view an app's title bar when in full-screen view. Not all apps have a hidden title bar to view.	
View the taskbar	▪ Swipe up from the bottom of the screen.	
Open, select, or activate an item	▪ Tap once on the item.	
Zoom in or out	▪ Touch the screen with two or more fingers and drag them away or toward from each other.	

Illustrations provided by GestureWorks® (www.gestureworks.com)

Check out the "Navigating with Gestures" link in the online resources (boostyourskills.lablearning.com) for more information.

Touchpad Controls

The touchpad on your laptop or device can do more than just point and click! The following special finger movements enhance your ability to control items on the screen:

USING TOUCH GESTURES		
Task	**Procedure**	
Open the Task screen	▪ Swipe three fingers upward on the touchpad.	
Show the Desktop	▪ Swipe three fingers downward on the touchpad.	
Switch between open windows	▪ Swipe three fingers right or left on the screen. This slowly flips between all open programs.	

Working with the Taskbar

The taskbar runs the width of the Desktop at the bottom of the screen. Icons for the Start menu and other default apps are centered on the taskbar, along with those for any apps you have opened.

Only one app window can be active at a time, and it will be displayed in front of the other inactive programs open on your Desktop. The active app button will have a highlighted, square background behind it. Clicking on an inactive app button will make that app active, and the computer will move its window in front of others on the Desktop.

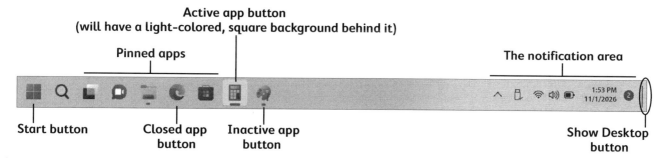

Active app button
(will have a light-colored, square background behind it)

Pinned apps

The notification area

Start button

Closed app button

Inactive app button

Show Desktop button

Notification Area

The notification area on the right end of the taskbar has four primary functions:

- It displays the system clock and current date.
- It displays icons representing tasks and functions that are running in the background, such as antivirus software.
- It displays notifications of system events, such as app updates.
- It provides access to some of the apps that have icons displayed.

HANDS-ON 2.4 Change Taskbar Settings

In this exercise, you will open the taskbar and the Start menu Properties dialog box to observe setting options and to make changes to the taskbar settings.

1. Follow these steps to display the Taskbar and Start menu Properties window:

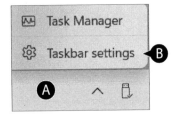

Ⓐ Right-click a clear portion of the taskbar to display its pop-up menu.

Ⓑ Choose **Taskbar Settings**.

2. Click the **On/Off** slider to the right of *Touch Keyboard* to turn on this feature.

This adds an icon to the taskbar that enables you to type by clicking a virtual keyboard on the screen.

3. Turn off the Touch Keyboard.

Notice that larger icons have been restored on the taskbar.

4. Close the Taskbar Settings window.

Pinning and Unpinning Apps

Windows allows you to pin app buttons to the taskbar in much the same way you pin programs to the Start menu. Pinning enables you to put your most-used apps on the taskbar where they are easier to find and launch. Typically, the taskbar is set to be displayed even when windows are maximized, which means that the pinned app buttons are always available. A pinned app that is not currently open will not have a square button border around its icon.

Pinned app buttons do not have borders when the app is closed.

PINNING AND UNPINNING PROGRAMS	
Task	**Procedure**
Pin an app	■ On the Start menu, right-click on the app button to display a pop-up menu. ■ Choose Pin to Taskbar. ■ The app button will remain on the taskbar even when the app is closed until it is unpinned.
Unpin an app	■ Right-click on the app button to display a pop-up menu. ■ Choose Unpin from Taskbar.

Tip! Having too many pinned apps on the taskbar can make it difficult to tell which programs are open and can cause confusion when you try to work with multiple apps.

HANDS-ON 2.5 Pin and Unpin an App

In this exercise, you will open Notepad, pin the app to the taskbar, and then unpin the app from the taskbar.

1. Click **Start** and click the **All Apps** button.

2. Scroll down through the apps and click **Notepad**.

3. Follow these steps to pin the app to the taskbar:

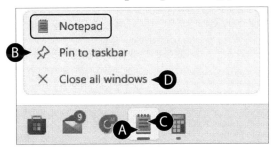

Ⓐ Right-click the app button on the taskbar.

Ⓑ Choose **Pin to Taskbar** from the menu.

Ⓒ Right-click the app button again.

Ⓓ Choose **Close All Windows** from the menu.

The Notepad icon remains on the taskbar. Once the app is closed, it no longer has a button border around it.

4. Follow these steps to unpin the Notepad app:

Ⓐ Right-click the app button.

Ⓑ Choose **Unpin from Taskbar**.

The Notepad icon is removed from the taskbar.

. . . .

Action Center (Notifications)

The Action Center provides a central location for information being shared by various apps in your computer. These notifications can be varied, from news alerts from your News app to updates from Windows.

The Action Center is accessed by clicking the Notification button in the notification area. It only appears when there are notifications to share.

⊞ + Ⓐ to open the Action Center

Notifications

Notifications vary depending on the app. When highlighted with your mouse, individual notifications can be deleted by using the Close button

Note! When you hover your mouse over the item, the close button appears on that item. The entire dialog box is closed by just clicking somewhere else on the screen.

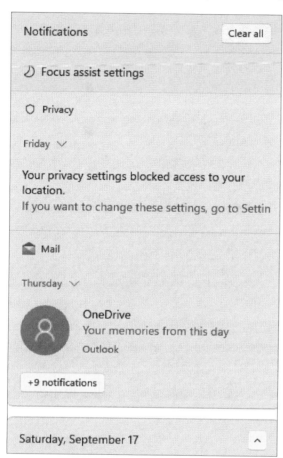

A specific section can be closed the same way. Notifications related to individual programs and various areas of Windows can be turned on and off in Settings.

HANDS-ON 2.6 Set Notifications

In this exercise, you will turn notifications off and then back on.

1. Choose **Start**→**Settings** and then click the **System** icon.

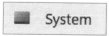

2. From the right side of the System window, choose **Notifications**.
   Notice that the Notification options slide onto the right side of the screen.

3. Click the **On/Off** slider to the right of *Get Notifications from Apps and Other Senders* to turn them off.

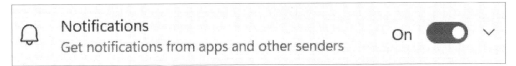

The Notification button is no longer visible on the taskbar.

4. Click the **On/Off** slider to the right of *Get Notifications from Apps and Other Senders* to turn notifications back on.

Scroll down through the Notifications window and notice you can turn notifications off for individual apps.

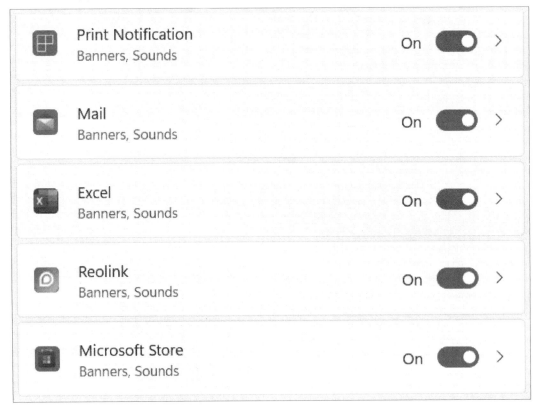

5. Close the Settings window.

Actions

The Action Center contains rows of icons, or actions, that enable you to quickly access various settings on your computer.

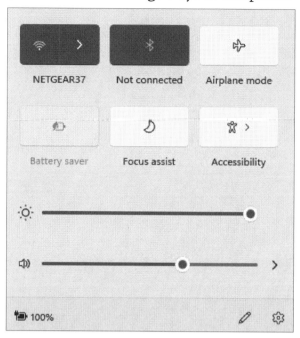

Using the Edit Quick Settings button (the pencil icon at the bottom of the screen), you can show additional actions and customize which actions will be shown.

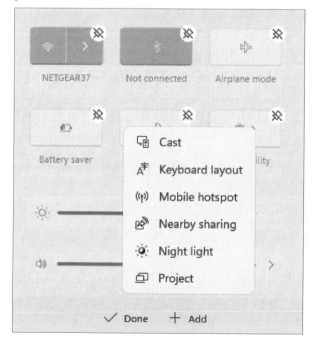

Multitasking

One useful feature of Windows is its ability to multitask. Multitasking enables the computer to run multiple programs or operations at the same time. Multitasking lets Windows run various tasks and activities in the background that you might not even be aware of, such as downloading software patches, monitoring the security of your computer, and performing hundreds of other small tasks. You also can take advantage of multitasking to help you to become more efficient with your time in front of the computer; you can have several programs open, check your email, pay bills online, listen to music, and print documents—all at the same time.

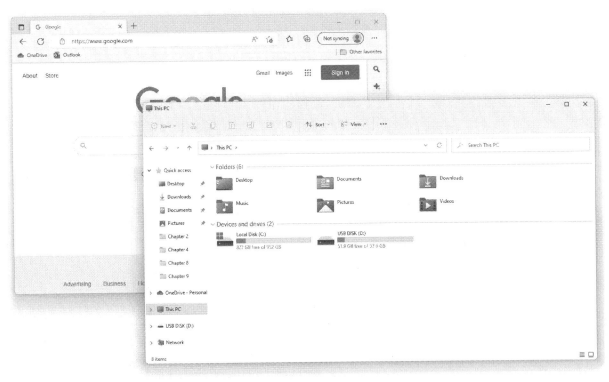

Multitasking lets you perform many tasks simultaneously: watch a video, shop online, view saved photos, and organize your files.

HANDS-ON 2.7 Open Multiple Programs

In this exercise, you will open three programs from the Start menu and watch the app buttons be added to the taskbar.

1. Click **Start**.

2. Click **Calculator** if available in the upper pane or choose it using the All Apps button.
   Notice the app button has been added to the taskbar.

3. Open Notepad from the All Apps listing.

4. Open Paint from the All Apps listing.

There are now three app buttons on the taskbar.

Leave these programs open for the next exercise.

App Switching

You can easily switch between open programs (when multitasking) using one of several switching tools. Windows often offers more than one way to complete a task. To make an app active, you can use the app window, the app button, the keyboard, or the Task View button.

Which App Is Active?

There is a rule when running multiple programs: You can work in only one app at a time. If you think of open app windows like objects on your desk, the object you are currently using would be the active object and would, most likely, be on top of the other objects.

Windows places the active app window in front (on top) of the inactive windows. The button will be brighter and will have a lighter background behind it and a long, blue bar under it.

The active app button is brighter.

Inactive buttons are darker in color and have a short, gray bar under them.

Tip! Open but inactive apps will have a short, gray bar under the bottom edge of their icons.

🖱 HANDS-ON 2.8 Switch Programs

In this exercise, you will change the active app window by clicking on inactive app windows and app buttons located on the taskbar.

Before You Begin: Three programs (Calculator, Notepad, and Paint) should still be open on the Desktop.

1. Follow these steps to make Calculator the active app:

Ⓐ If necessary, restore down, resize, and move the windows to approximate the way they look here.

Ⓑ If Calculator is not active, click the **Calculator** app button to make it the active app.

2. Follow these steps to change the active app:

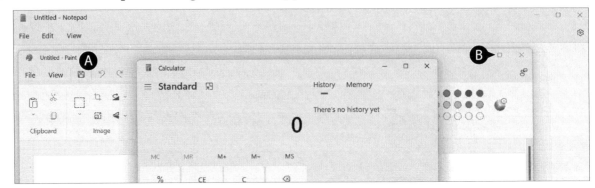

Ⓐ Click a visible part of the Paint window to make the window and the app button active.

Ⓑ Click the **Maximize** button to make the Paint window cover the Desktop.

Ⓒ Although Paint is hiding the other programs, click the **Calculator** app button to make it active.

If any part of an inactive window can be seen, clicking the window will make it active, but avoid clicking its Close button! If windows are maximized, use the app buttons to make other programs active.

3. Make Notepad active and click the **Close** button to exit the app.

Leave Calculator and Paint open.

The Flip Command

The **Flip** command enables you to quickly switch or "flip" between open programs. You access the command using the keyboard.

> Alt + Tab to switch between open programs

Tip! The Flip command is the quickest way to switch between open programs while keeping your hands on the keyboard.

SWITCHING PROGRAMS USING FLIP	
Task	Procedure
Use the Flip command	▪ Hold down Alt and tap Tab to display the Flip window. ▪ While continuing to hold down Alt, keep tapping Tab until the icon for the app you want to use is selected. ▪ Release Alt. The app window you chose is now active.

HANDS-ON 2.9 Flip Between Active Programs

In this exercise, you will flip (switch) between Calculator, Paint, and the Notepad.

1. Start Notepad.

2. Make Paint the active app if it is inactive.

3. Hold down the Alt key on the keyboard and keep it held down until step 5. (Use your left thumb so you can tap the Tab key in the next step.)

4. Tap the Tab key once (while continuing to hold down Alt).

The Task-Switching box appears. The order of the icons for open programs can be different and will change depending on which app was active when you gave the Flip command.

5. While holding down the $\boxed{Alt}$ key, tap the $\boxed{Tab}$ key until **Calculator** is chosen in the Task Switcher window.

6. Release the $\boxed{Alt}$ key.
   The Calculator app becomes active and jumps to the front of the Desktop.

7. Practice using $\boxed{Alt}$ + $\boxed{Tab}$ to switch between programs.
   Leave Calculator, Notepad, and Paint open.

. . . .

Show Desktop and Task View

Windows provides other features to help you navigate between multiple windows in quick and efficient ways:

Show Desktop button—The Show Desktop button is located at the far right end of the taskbar. It helps you quickly clear the Desktop of window clutter because instead of minimizing one window at a time, you can minimize all windows at the same time.

Task View button—The Task View button enables you to choose among your open apps without having to hold down multiple buttons on the keyboard like Flip requires.

When the Task View button is clicked on the taskbar, a screen showing all open apps appears, including a live view of what's running in each app. Clicking on a specific app makes it live on the screen.

HANDS-ON 2.10 Use Task View

In this exercise, you will use the Task View button to switch between running apps.
Before You Begin: Three apps (Calculator, Notepad, and Paint) should still be open on the Desktop.

1. Click on the **Paint** app to make it the active app.

2. Click the **Task View** button on the taskbar.

3. Click **Calculator** in the Task View window.
   Notice that the Calculator app is now the active app on the Desktop.

4. Practice using the Task View button to switch between open apps.

5. Close the Calculator, Notepad, and Paint apps.

· ·

The Usefulness of Multitasking

Multitasking—the ability to perform more than one task at a time—is a powerful tool. Coupled with today's sophisticated processors, large monitors, and Windows' new features, multitasking can make your work time more efficient and your personal time more fun.

Before the advent of Microsoft Windows, PCs could run only one app at a time. If you were printing a long document from an older PC, you had to wait for the job to finish before you could check your email or continue playing Solitaire.

Windows has increased multitasking capabilities over its predecessors that enable a multitude of processes to run in the background, such as antivirus protection, automatic updates, and messaging. At the same time, you can be printing a document, downloading a movie from the Internet, catching up on your email, and listening to music.

Multitasking allows you to perform many tasks simultaneously, such as checking email, paying bills online, listening to music, and printing documents.

Self-Assessment

To check your knowledge of the key concepts introduced in this chapter, complete this Self-Assessment quiz.

1. Touch gestures are special finger movements used with the touchscreen on a laptop. **true false**

2. Multitasking enables you to run more than one app at a time. **true false**

3. The Show Desktop button maximizes all open apps. **true false**

4. If you open three programs, you will have three active app windows. **true false**

5. Task View allows you to choose between apps without holding down multiple keyboard buttons. **true false**

6. Using the Minimize, Maximize, and Restore Down buttons to resize a window is called multitasking. **true false**

7. Which is NOT a quick-sizing button?

   A. ×

   B. −

   C. □

   D. ⧉

   E. None of the above

8. Which button minimizes a window?

   A. ×

   B. −

   C. □

   D. ⧉

   E. None of the above

9. How can you tell if an app is active?

   A. Its window is the biggest.

   B. Its name is grayed out in the title bar.

   C. Its app button looks brighter on the taskbar.

   D. All of the above

10. Which is NOT a touch gesture?

    A. Open task view

    B. Zoom in

    C. Open help app

    D. Zoom out

Skill Builders

Resize and Move Apps

In this exercise, you will resize and move the Calculator on the Desktop.

1. Start the Calculator app.

2. Maximize the app using the **Maximize** button.

3. Restore down the Calculator app.

4. Click in the title bar of Calculator and drag it to a new position on the screen.

5. Minimize the Calculator window.

6. Click the **Calculator** button on the taskbar to restore it to the Desktop.

7. Close the Calculator app.

Pin and Unpin Apps

In this exercise, you will pin two commands to the Start menu and use commands to launch both apps. Finally, you will unpin the commands from the Start menu.

1. Choose **Start→All Apps**.

2. Right-click the **Notepad** and **Paint** items to pin these commands to the Pinned area of the Start menu.

Launch Pinned Programs

3. Launch Notepad using the new icon.

4. Launch Paint using the new Paint icon.
   Leave the programs open on the Desktop for the next exercise.

Remove the New Commands

5. Click **Start**.

6. Right-click the **Notepad** icon and the **Paint** icon and unpin their icons from the Start menu's Pinned area.

7. Dismiss the Start menu.

In this exercise, you will multitask by using the control features discussed in this chapter.

Before You Begin: Notepad and Paint should still be open.

1. Click the **Notepad** app button on the taskbar to make it active.

   Notepad jumps in front of the other window, and its title bar changes to show it is the active app. Also notice that Notepad's taskbar button appears brighter than the other app's button.

2. Click the **Paint** app button on the taskbar to make it active.

3. **Maximize** the Paint window.

   Let's say you want to make Notepad the active app again. Because Notepad is hidden under Paint, you need to use its taskbar button to make the app active.

4. Click the **Notepad** app button on the taskbar to make Notepad active.

   The Notepad window pops up on top of the Paint window, ready for you to type in it.

5. **Maximize** the Notepad window.

6. **Restore Down** each app.

   Each app now has a window size that partially fills the Desktop.

7. Practice resizing and moving each app window.

8. Minimize both programs at the same time using the **Show Desktop** button at the right end of the taskbar.

   The purpose of the Show Desktop button is to minimize all open programs with a single click, giving you quick access to the Desktop.

9. Follow these steps to quickly close the minimized Notepad app:

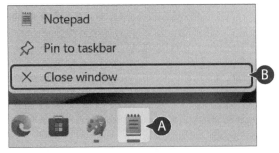

   Ⓐ Right-click the app button to display the control menu.

   Ⓑ Choose **Close Window**.

10. Use the same right-click method on the Paint taskbar button to close its window.

CHAPTER 3

Creating an Online Account

LEARNING OBJECTIVES

- Describe why we use online resources
- Understand the basics of cloud computing
- Create a free Microsoft account
- Connect your Microsoft account to Windows
- Understand account verification

Online apps give you the ability to work anywhere on any computer or device, such as a phone or tablet. With online storage, you can also access your files anywhere from any device that is linked to the Internet. In this chapter, you will learn about online apps and storage. You'll also set up your own free Microsoft account.

Learning Resources: **boostyourskills.lablearning.com**

📂 Case Study: Going Online

Dave was upset. His new computer didn't have any apps to help him get his schoolwork done, and he didn't have any money left to purchase any.

Dave's friend Greg suggested that Dave get a free Microsoft account. "With a Microsoft account, you can access many great apps straight from the Internet at no cost," Greg said. "The apps are not as powerful as the ones you would purchase, but they help you get your schoolwork done."

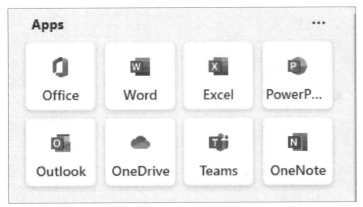

The various apps available when you sign up for a Microsoft account

Dave set up his Microsoft account and was surprised by everything he was able to do. Soon, Dave was creating documents and presentations and receiving email. He was also able to store all his files online.

It didn't take long for Dave to become a productive online app–using student!

Note! This is a special chapter designed to get you signed up for a Microsoft account that can be used throughout the remainder of this book. This chapter is shorter than the others and does not contain the Skill Builder exercises used in the other chapters.

Why Online?

The Internet has grown from a tool for sending messages and doing research into a vast system with unlimited possibilities. As the access to and size of online storage have expanded exponentially, access speeds have increased and the number of access points has multiplied. As a result, you now are able to store all your apps, documents, music, pictures, video, and more online and also access your work from any computer or device that's connected to the Internet.

The Cloud

The cloud, or **cloud computing**, generally refers to the storage of apps and services on the Internet so they can be accessed from anywhere by your computers and devices that have Internet access. Many of the apps in Windows 11 are cloud based and require a connection to the Internet to function.

There are many online **cloud storage** providers, including Microsoft OneDrive, Dropbox, Google Drive, box, and more.

The logos for four popular cloud storage sites: Microsoft OneDrive, Dropbox, Google Drive, and box

Microsoft 365 for the Web

Microsoft offers a number of apps that are completely online—and free. They include online storage with OneDrive and a suite of programs simply called Microsoft 365 (previously named Office Online). With these tools, you can work on your documents and files, store your files online, and access them from any computer or device, including your smartphone! These online apps are free to use, and some of them are used in this book.

The Microsoft 365 online apps (Microsoft may refer to them as "Office for the web" apps) offer basic functionality, and more complete versions can be purchased if needed.

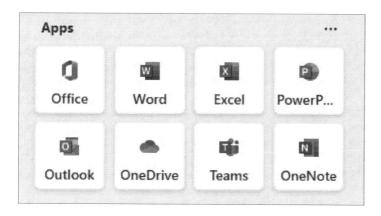

Creating Your Microsoft Account

Creating an online Microsoft account is simple and will enable you to complete many of the exercises in this book. If you have Windows already installed on a home computer or have used one of the many Microsoft online services, you may already have an account.

If you already have a Microsoft account, use that account in this chapter and throughout this book.

Account Verification

Once your account information has been accepted, Microsoft may send a verification to your email address. This is a security check to make sure you are the one who created the account.

Clicking the verify link in the email completes the verification process and unlocks all the features of your Microsoft account.

ACCOUNTS AND APPS	
Account/App	**What Is It For?**
Windows login	Sign on to the computer
Microsoft account	Allows access to OneDrive and Microsoft 365 for the web; needs to be connected with your Windows login
OneDrive	Microsoft's free online storage option and the starting point for accessing Microsoft 365 apps in this book
Microsoft 365 for the web	Free basic versions of some of Microsoft's apps

HANDS-ON 3.1 Create a Microsoft Account

In this exercise, you will create a Microsoft account that will be used throughout this book.

Before You Begin: Make sure you have an email address that you can use and check.

1. Start the Microsoft Edge browser by clicking the icon on the taskbar.

2. **Maximize** the browser window.

3. In the address bar, type **account.microsoft.com** and tap ⌘Enter⌘.

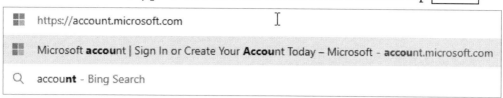

4. Click the **Create a Microsoft Account** link.

   This page will change periodically, so the link may not always be in the same location. At the time of this writing, it's toward the top of the page and near the Sign In button.

5. Enter your email address and click **Next**.

6. Enter a password for your new Microsoft account, using the same password you use to log in to Windows and click **Next**.
   Leave Microsoft Edge open.

Tip!   Write down your password as a reminder in case you forget it later.

7. Enter your country/region and your birth date using the drop-down fields and then click **Next**.

Verify Your Account

8. Access your email and look for a new email from the Microsoft account team.

9. Enter the code that was sent to you into the Verify Email dialog box.

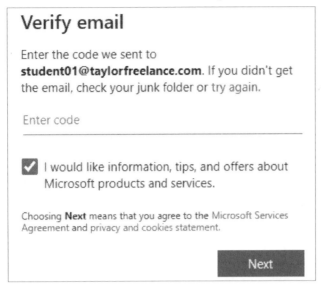

10. Click **Next**. If asked, solve the puzzle seen in the box (it doesn't always appear) and then click **Next**.

11. Click **Next**.

   You will be taken to your account screen, which contains all the information about your online Microsoft account.

Making Connections

Your Microsoft account must be connected to the Windows login you use to sign on to the computer. This connection allows Windows to automatically connect you to various apps without constantly asking for your login information. Many of the apps that come with Windows will automatically connect to your Microsoft account as well.

HANDS-ON 3.2 Connect Accounts

In this exercise, you will connect your newly created Microsoft account to your Windows login.

Before You Begin: Make sure you are logged in with your login.

1. In the Start menu, click your **user icon/name** button and then click **Change Account Settings**.

2. Click the **Your Info** button on the right side of the screen, if necessary.

3. Click the **Sign In with a Microsoft Account** link.

4. Enter your email and click **Next**.

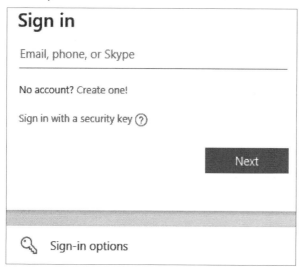

5. Enter your Microsoft account password and click **Sign In**.

6. Enter your Windows login password and click **Next**.

Sign into this computer using your Microsoft account

Next time you sign into this computer, use your Microsoft account password or Windows Hello, if you've set it up.

We'll need your current Windows password one last time.

Current Windows password

Next

7. Click **Skip for Now** when asked if you want to sign in using your face.

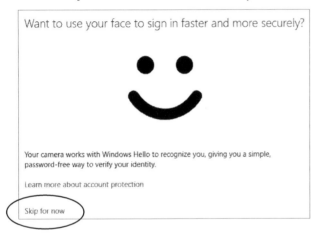

Want to use your face to sign in faster and more securely?

Your camera works with Windows Hello to recognize you, giving you a simple, password-free way to verify your identity.

Learn more about account protection

Skip for now

8. Click **Next** in the prompt window and, in the next window, set up your PIN and click **OK**. (A PIN enables you to log in with a simpler login, much like your ATM code.)

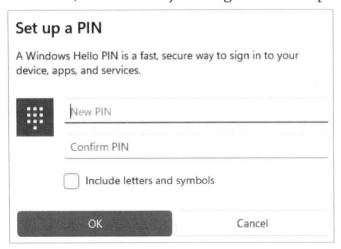

Set up a PIN

A Windows Hello PIN is a fast, secure way to sign in to your device, apps, and services.

New PIN

Confirm PIN

☐ Include letters and symbols

OK   Cancel

Your Microsoft account is now connected to your Windows login credentials.

9. Close the account window.

· ·

Logging In to OneDrive and Microsoft 365 for the Web

Now that you have a Microsoft account, you can use it to log in to OneDrive and Microsoft 365 for the web. OneDrive is your online file storage and the starting point for logging in to the other online Microsoft 365 apps that are used in this book.

Online Messages

When using a browser and online apps, you may get messages on the screen that are not part of the content of this book but rather a normal part of the online experience.

Would you like to save your password for live.com?
More info

Yes   No   ✕

Sometimes the browser will ask if you want to save the password you have just entered. In most cases, you will want to click No and continue on with your work.

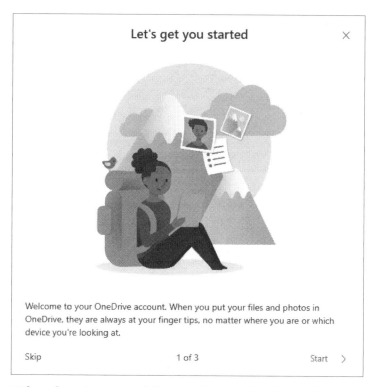

Let's get you started   ✕

Welcome to your OneDrive account. When you put your files and photos in OneDrive, they are always at your finger tips, no matter where you are or which device you're looking at.

Skip   1 of 3   Start >

When logging in to Microsoft 365 for the web apps, you may get a "What's New" or other message that will tell you about new features that have been added. These messages can be closed by clicking the Close button on the top-right corner of the dialog box.

Tip! It's common for messages to show up on the screen. After reading them, click Close or OK.

HANDS-ON 3.3 Log In to OneDrive

In this exercise, you will log in to OneDrive. This is the process you will follow each time.

Before You Begin: Make sure you have created a Microsoft account in Hands-On 3.1 and have the login and password from that exercise.

1. If necessary, start the Microsoft Edge browser by clicking the icon on the taskbar.

2. If necessary, **Maximize** the browser window.

3. Type **onedrive.live.com** in the address bar and tap ⌨Enter⌨.

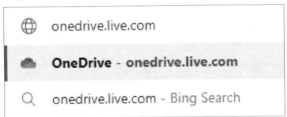

Are You Already Logged In?

If you have connected your Microsoft account to your Windows login, you may find that you are already logged in to OneDrive. Use these steps to verify that your Microsoft account is the one that is being used.

4. Click the **No Thanks** button to close any advertisements for purchasing more storage space, if they appear.

5. Click the **user icon/name** button on the right-hand side of OneDrive and verify whether you are logged in.

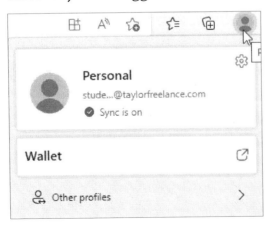

- If it's your login, awesome! Go to step 9.
- If it's not your login, click **Sign Out** and go to step 6.
- If no one is logged in and OneDrive is not open, go to step 6.

Basic Login

If you are signing in as a guest on Windows or have not yet connected your Windows account to your Windows login, you will start the sign-in process at the "splash" screen for OneDrive.

6. Click the **Sign In** button in the top-right corner of the OneDrive screen.

7. Enter the email address you used for your Microsoft account and click **Next**.

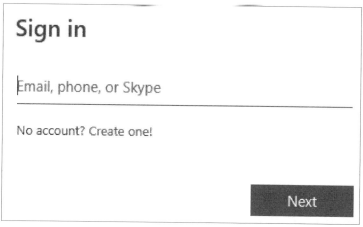

8. Enter your password and click **Sign In**.

9. When done with OneDrive, click the **Close** button to exit Microsoft Edge.

Always Logged In

Once you have created your Microsoft account and opened OneDrive, Windows should remember your login and automatically start OneDrive when accessed. You should only have to use your login and password in these situations:

- When accessing OneDrive from a public access computer, such as one in a library, copy shop, or hotel business office
- When your Microsoft account is not connected to your login
- When using any computer or device that is not your own

Opening Microsoft 365 for the Web Apps

Once you have logged in to OneDrive, you can open any of the Microsoft 365 online apps by clicking the app launcher located on the left side of the online app's title bar. All Microsoft 365 online apps feature an app launcher.

The app launcher lists all of the Microsoft services you have access to. Clicking a service on the app launcher starts a new browser tab with that app running in it.

HANDS-ON 3.4 Start the Word Online App

In this exercise, you will go to OneDrive online and start the Word online app.

1. Start the Microsoft Edge browser by clicking its icon on the taskbar.

2. **Maximize** the browser window.

3. Type **onedrive.live.com** in the address bar and tap ⌐Enter⌐.

4. Log in to OneDrive if not already logged in.
   Refer to Hands-On 3.3 if you need a reminder about doing this.

5. Click the **app launcher** on the left side of the OneDrive title bar and choose **Word** from the menu that appears.

Notice that the browser now says "Word" instead of "OneDrive."

Note! Remember, if the "What's New" window appears, simply click Got It! to close.

6. Choose the **New Blank Document** option.

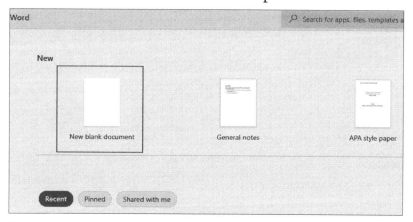

You are now in Word and are ready to write.

7. Exit Microsoft Edge using the **Close** button. This also closes Word, which is open within the browser window.

. . . .

Self-Assessment

To check your knowledge of the key concepts introduced in this chapter, complete this Self-Assessment quiz.

1. The cloud refers to the Wi-Fi network in your home.   **true false**

2. Account verification makes sure you are the one who created the Microsoft account.   **true false**

3. Windows remembers your login and automatically starts OneDrive when accessed.   **true false**

4. By connecting your Microsoft account to Windows, many additional apps will be able to connect to your account automatically.   **true false**

5. Storing your files in the cloud allows you to access them from anywhere.   **true false**

6. Which app is NOT a free app that your Microsoft Account gives you access to?

    A. Excel

    B. Publisher

    C. Word

    D. Outlook

7. When do you need to log in to OneDrive?

    A. When a guest on a friend's computer

    B. When accessing from a browser in the library

    C. When your Microsoft account is not connected to your login

    D. All of the above

Working with Apps

LEARNING OBJECTIVES

- Use common features found in drop-down menus, on toolbars and Ribbons, and on scroll bars

- Use the mouse effectively as the appearance and function of the mouse pointer changes

- Type and edit text in an app

- Cut or copy text and then paste it into another location

- Save files or copies of files on OneDrive

In this chapter, you will explore two apps: a picture drawing and editing program called Paint and an online word-processing program called Word. As you use these very different programs, you will learn about the similarities and differences between their program controls, including menus, toolbars, Ribbons, mouse pointers, and scroll bars. You also will learn widely used computer skills and program concepts, including typing and editing text on a computer; cutting, copying, and pasting text; and saving your creations online on Microsoft OneDrive. Keep in mind as you work through this chapter that while some of the skills and features are unique to these programs, many are also part of the standard features found in other Windows programs.

Learning Resources: **boostyourskills.lablearning.com**

📂 Case Study: Creating a Letter Including a Map

Sylvia wants to start a small home-based business. Her hobby for years has been raising goldfish. She thinks there is an untapped market in her area for setting up small aquariums in offices and providing aquarium maintenance services. To test the market, Sylvia wants to send letters and deliver flyers to local businesses explaining the products and services her business provides. She needs a small map to add to the letters, but like many small start-up businesses, she doesn't have a lot of money. She decides to use the Maps app that comes with Windows along with the built-in snipping tool to take screen captures. She types her letters in Word and is then able to copy the map and paste it into her letters.

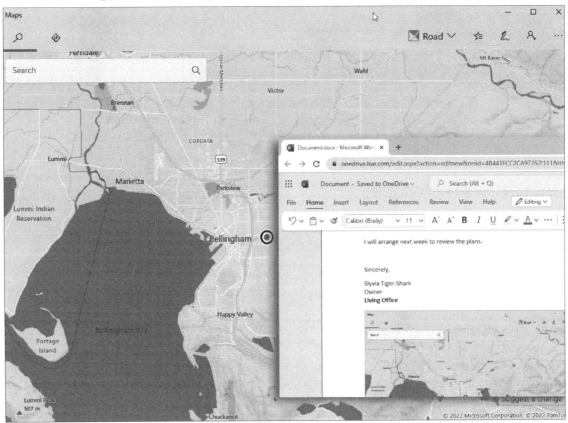

Maps, a mapping program, and Word, a word-processing program

App Commands

Within apps, commands have traditionally been accessed from a series of drop-down menus on a menu bar or command buttons on a toolbar. Starting with Office 2007, Microsoft introduced the "Windows Ribbon framework" in some of its programs as a new way to display commands, and most apps now use the **Ribbon** feature.

Menu Commands

Drop-down menus are featured in older Windows-based programs, such as Notepad. Menus are lists of commands traditionally organized in a series along a menu bar under the title bar. The first menu on most menu bars is the File menu, the second is the Edit menu, and the last is the Help menu.

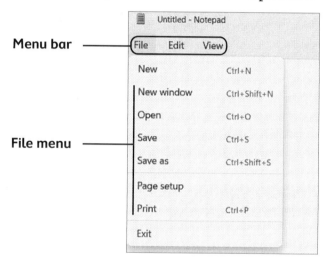

Apps that use the Ribbon system to display commands do not use drop-down menus. Instead, commands are organized into tabs that open in the Ribbon. The File menu may still use a drop-down menu or open a completely new screen called a program stage depending on the app and the amount of information that needs to be displayed.

Ribbon with Home tab showing

Many of the commands in Notepad's File menu are standard to most programs, including Word. On the other hand, File Explorer (a file-management app) has commands related to managing files and folders that do not appear in the menus of Notepad or Word.

Tip! Menu commands do not always appear in the same order in different programs, and the text labels can vary.

🖱 HANDS-ON 4.1 Compare Drop-Down Menus

In this exercise, you will launch Notepad and Paint. You will compare common features in the File and Edit drop-down menus in these programs.

1. Click **Start** and choose **All Apps**. Click **Notepad**.

2. Repeat step 1, but this time launch Paint.

3. Use the taskbar to make Notepad the active program window.

4. Follow the steps below to access the File drop-down menu:

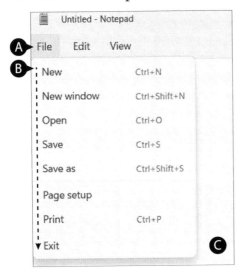

Ⓐ Click **File** on the menu bar to access the menu.

Ⓑ Taking care not to click anything, run your mouse pointer over the commands to momentarily highlight each one.

Ⓒ Dismiss the menu by clicking in a clear area outside the menu but within the Notepad window.

5. Make Paint the active program and then repeat step 3 with the Paint menu to see how it is similar to and different from Notepad's File menu.
   Notice that the menus have common features, including New, Open, Save, Save As, Print, and Exit.

6. Compare Notepad's traditional Edit menu with Paint's new default Ribbon, which holds the Cut, Copy, and Paste commands.

7. Click **Close** to exit Notepad, but leave Paint open.

Commands in Programs with Ribbons

Two of the programs used in this book, Paint and Word, use Ribbons to display commands. These commands are divided among a number of tabs.

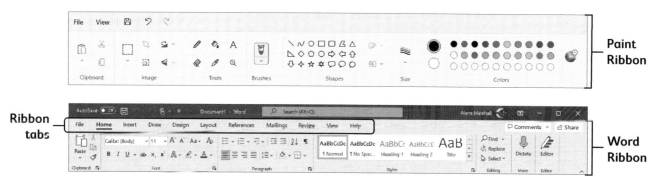

Both of these Ribbons have been designed to help the user create files. They each have tools specific to the program's function (e.g., Paint is used to create and edit pictures, and Word is used to create and edit text), and they each share a common feature of organizing tools into categories.

Quick Access Toolbar

A toolbar is used to display series of commands as small buttons or drop-down lists. Commands on a toolbar or Ribbon are often referred to as "tools." The **Quick Access toolbar** typically has three tools displayed: Save, Undo, and Redo.

The Quick Access toolbar will also have a drop-down menu that enables you to add commands to the toolbar.

Ribbon Tabs

Paint has only one Ribbon. Word and some other programs have many more tabs.

A Ribbon contains many tools. Tabs on the Ribbon are used to arrange tools by task. On each tab, related tools are assembled into command groups. Each command group has vertical separators and a label. Within each group, tools can be displayed as buttons, drop-down lists, or **galleries** of options from which to choose.

The icon for each tool attempts to indicate its purpose, but you can use your mouse pointer to hover over a tool to display its name in a ScreenTip.

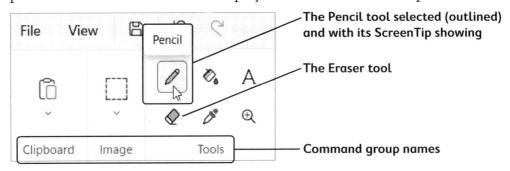

Tip! If you are new to computers and feel uncomfortable using a mouse, try drawing pictures and then carefully erasing lines in Paint. This is a fun and easy way to improve your mouse skills.

HANDS-ON 4.2 Draw in the Paint App

In this exercise, you will draw a face and sign your name using the Pencil tool in Paint.

1. Follow these steps to use the Pencil tool:

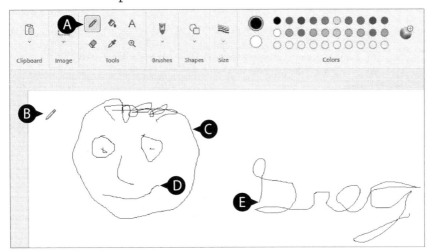

Ⓐ Click once on the **Pencil** tool to select it.

Ⓑ Point with the mouse pointer over the white canvas in the drawing area. The mouse pointer will now look like a pencil.

Ⓒ Drag (hold down the left mouse button and move) the Pencil in a circle to draw a rough circle for a face. Release the mouse button once you've drawn the circle.

Ⓓ Drag the Pencil to draw other parts of the face. Release the mouse button after completing each part.

Ⓔ Try signing your name by dragging using the Pencil.

You will save your work in the next exercise.

If you don't like what you've drawn, choose the Eraser tool from the Tools group, drag to erase, and then choose the Pencil to try again.

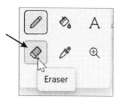

Saving Your Work

When you type a letter or create a drawing as you did in the previous exercise, you usually want to save it so you can look at or work on it again later, but the computer does not save your work unless you command it to do so. Remember that if you save it to OneDrive, you can view it on any machine or device.

This section looks at two commands used to save your work: Save and Save As.

Saving your work frequently also protects you from any sudden computer failure or loss of power.

Where Your Work Is Located

In Chapter 1, "Getting Your First Look," you learned that all of the things displayed on your screen are temporarily stored in the RAM chips of the computer. The work you have done so far in Paint is only temporarily stored in RAM, and if the power were to go out or someone were to shut down the computer, your work would be lost.

You must therefore save your work on a permanent storage device, such as a hard drive or a USB flash drive, or online to OneDrive to keep it from being erased. See "Behind the Screen: Drive Designations" for descriptions of storage devices.

Windows needs to know two things the first time you save your work:

- What do you want to call it?
- Where do you want to store it?

Files and Folders

These two basic terms, files and folders, will be covered in more detail in Chapter 6, "Finding Files," but they need to be defined here:

- **File**—A collection of data stored with a name. Examples of files are a letter you've typed and saved, a drawing in Paint that you've saved, or a picture copied from the Internet.

- **Folder**—An electronic location in which you store related groups of files. For example, Pictures and Documents are folders already created for your username in Windows in which you can store photos and other files.

Choosing a Storage Location

Today's computers provide a variety of storage options, including internal and external hard drives, DVDs, USB flash drives, and online locations, like OneDrive, Google Drive, and others, which you were introduced to in Chapter 3, "Creating an Online Account." When you are ready to save, you choose which storage device you want to use. And remember, if you don't choose, the computer will choose for you (using what is called a *default* setting).

The Internal Hard Drive

When saving your work (file) for the first time, most Windows programs will direct you to a predetermined location (folder) on the internal hard drive. On your home computer:

- Notepad directs you to the Documents folder.
- Paint directs you to the Pictures folder.

Using the predetermined location is usually appropriate for new users until they learn more about the Windows storage system, which is covered in Chapter 6, "Finding Files."

A Portable USB Flash Drive

You can choose a different location for saving from the one chosen by a program. USB flash drives (also called *thumb, pen,* or *keychain drives*) are a convenient storage method that make it easy to access files from different computers and locations.

A flash drive is a device with a USB plug attached to a storage card. The flash drive can be plugged into any USB port on a computer.

Connecting a flash drive to a computer

OneDrive

You can choose to save your files to OneDrive (your cloud storage), which is just as easy to do as saving your work to your USB flash drive. By saving online, your files are accessible on any computer or device with an Internet connection and browser. This is the preferred method when using this book and is the one shown in most exercises.

Filenames

Data that is stored on a storage device is called a file. A file might contain a text document, a picture, a song, a movie, or any other kind of data. The first time you store data, it must be given a filename. The filename must follow Windows' file-naming conventions (rules):

NAMING FILES	
Convention	**Description**
Filename length	Up to 255 characters
Allowed characters	All alphanumeric characters except those that are reserved (see below)
Reserved characters	| \ ? * < " : > /
Reserved words	CON, PRN, AUX, NUL, COM1 (2-9), LPT1 (2-9)

Tip! Choose a filename that will help you recognize the file's contents months from now. A filename like *Sales Letter to Business Offices* is more useful than *Sales Letter.* If possible, keep the length less than 20 characters or so to make the name easier to read in various windows and dialog boxes.

Save Versus Save As

The first time you save a document with the Save command, Windows opens a Save As dialog box asking for a filename and a storage location. After a file has been saved, choosing the Save command will save the changes without opening a dialog box because Windows already knows the filename and location.

The Save As command is also used to save a copy of a file in three ways:

- It lets you save an existing file with a different name (leaving the original file intact).
- It lets you save an existing file to another location (the filename can be the same or different).
- It lets you save an existing file in a different format, like PDF.

HANDS-ON 4.3 Save a New Document

Saving protects your work from a power failure or other loss. In this exercise, you will save your Paint picture to your hard drive, your USB flash drive, and to OneDrive. While you normally will save to just one storage location, here you are practicing saving to multiple locations.

Before You Begin: Paint should still be open.

1. If necessary, make Paint the active program window.

2. Click the **File** tab and choose **Save**.

Paint opens a Save As dialog box the first time a document is saved. Notice that Paint directs you to a folder (in this example, Pictures) and has provided a temporary filename, Untitled.

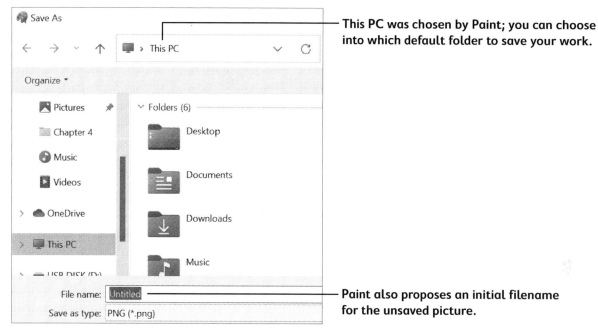

This PC was chosen by Paint; you can choose into which default folder to save your work.

Paint also proposes an initial filename for the unsaved picture.

In the next step, you will choose a storage location for your file.

In steps 3–7, you will practice saving the file to three different storage locations. Normally you will save to just one location.

Save to the Hard Drive

3. If necessary, double-click the default filename to select it and then type **My Signature** and click **Save**.

Paint saves your file to the hard drive. The new filename is displayed on the title bar.

Save to a USB Flash Drive

4. Choose **File**→**Save As**→**PNG Picture**.

5. Follow these steps to save your file to a USB flash drive:

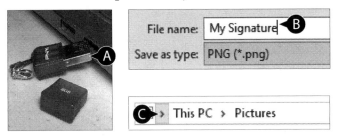

Ⓐ Place your USB flash drive into a USB port on the front or back of the computer, or perhaps into a cable. Ask for help, if necessary.

Ⓑ If necessary, double-click the default filename to select it and then type:

My Signature

Ⓒ Click the first drop-down list ⟩ button on the address bar to open the menu.

Drop-down list buttons often show a right-pointing arrow ⟩ *that, when clicked, becomes a downward-pointing arrow* ⌄.

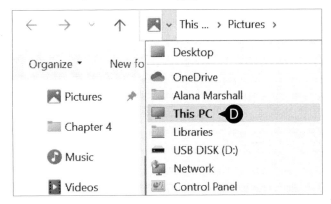

Ⓓ Choose **This PC**.

Ⓔ Click the second drop-down list ⌄ button.

Ⓕ Choose your USB flash drive (the drive name/letter will likely differ from what's shown). Click **Save**.

A copy of My Signature is saved on your flash drive.

Save to OneDrive

6. Choose **File→Save As→PNG Picture**.

7. Follow these steps to save your file to OneDrive:

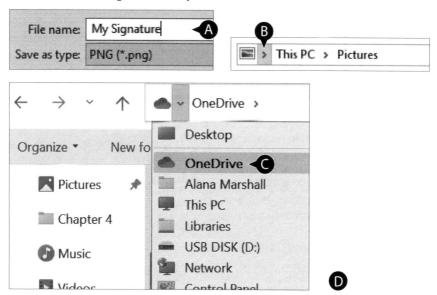

Ⓐ If necessary, double-click the default filename to select it and then type:

My Signature

Ⓑ Click the first drop-down list 〉button on the address bar to open the menu.

Ⓒ Choose **OneDrive**.

Ⓓ Click **Save** or tap ⸢Enter⸥ on the keyboard.

A copy of My Signature is saved on OneDrive. You now have three copies of the file, each saved to a different storage location.

8. Close Paint.

. . . .

The Work Area

Up to this point, you have concentrated on features on the perimeter of program windows, such as borders, menus, and control buttons. These are the tools that help when you are working in a program. Now you will look more closely at the work area, the place where you use the tools and do the work.

Mouse Pointers

In the last exercise, you saw that the mouse pointer looked like a pencil when the Pencil tool was active. In Windows, the appearance of the mouse pointer changes as the functions or capabilities of the mouse pointer change.

WINDOWS MOUSE POINTERS	
Mouse Pointer	**Function**
⌖	Normal selection pointer
I	Text selection pointer
╬	Precision selection pointer
✥	Move pointer
⟺	Horizontal resize pointer
⤢	Diagonal resize pointer
↕	Vertical resize pointer

Tool Galleries

Many tool groups in Paint include galleries, which are collections of tools or options. Tools in a gallery may be shown in full or partial view, or they may be hidden from view as a button on the Ribbon. If only part of the gallery is visible, a scroll bar is provided to view the remaining tools. If a gallery is hidden, its gallery button will display a downward-pointing arrow, which must be **selected** in order to display its drop-down gallery.

Tip! Users new to a program with a Ribbon will find it easier to use the Ribbon if the program window is maximized. Some tool groups and galleries change to buttons as the window is made smaller.

Paint will remember the most recently selected options the next time you use that tool. Also, be aware that when different tools are selected, options such as line thickness in the Size gallery can change.

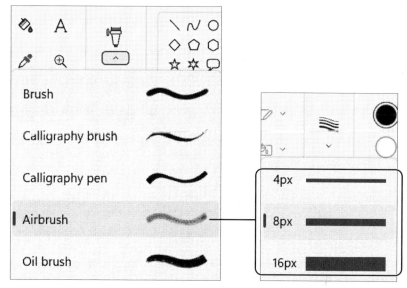

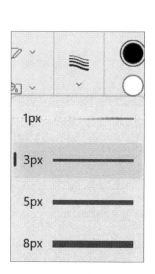

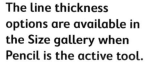

The line thickness options are available in the Size gallery when Pencil is the active tool.

Airbrush is the selected tool in this drop-down Brushes gallery.

The size options are different when Airbrush is made the active tool.

HANDS-ON 4.4 Change Mouse Pointers in Paint

In this exercise, you will select different tools from the Paint program Ribbon and observe appearance changes in the mouse pointer as you create a drawing.

1. Choose **Start →All Apps→Paint**.

2. **Maximize** the window.

3. Click the buttons in the Tools group one at a time and move your mouse over the white canvas to see the mouse pointer.
   Notice the changing appearance of the mouse pointer.

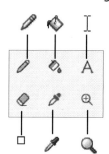

4. Follow these step-by-step options for the Rectangle tool:

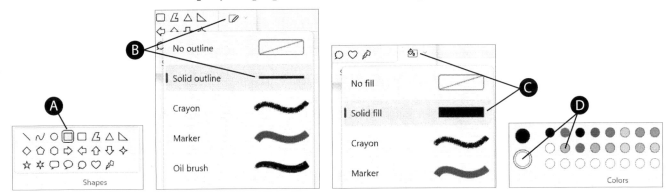

Ⓐ Choose the **Rectangle** tool from the Shapes gallery.

Ⓑ Click the **Outline** tool and choose **Solid Outline**.

Ⓒ Click the **Fill** tool and choose **Solid Fill**.

Ⓓ Click the **Color 2** tool and choose **Light Gray**.

5. Point near the top of the drawing area and then drag down and to the right to make a box.

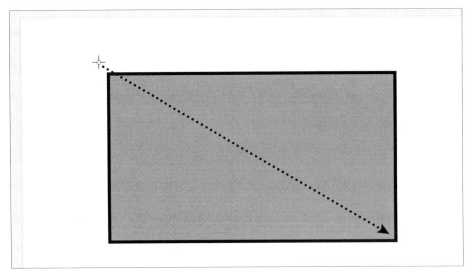

The line color is determined by the Color 1 choice; the fill color is determined by the Color 2 choice.

6. Follow these steps to set up and use the Eraser tool:

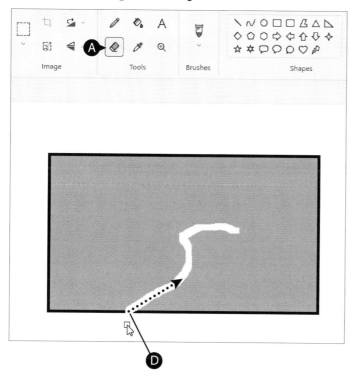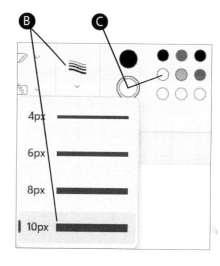

Ⓐ Choose the **Eraser** tool.

Ⓑ Pick any size for the eraser from the Size gallery.

Ⓒ Click **Color 2** and choose **White** as the background color.

Ⓓ Drag with the **Eraser** tool to erase part of the box.

Notice that the mouse pointer changes to reflect the size and color of the Eraser. The Eraser tool does not actually erase; rather, it paints using what you chose as Color 2.

7. Leave Paint open for the next exercise.

Scroll Bars

When part of your picture or content is too large to be seen in the app window, Windows will display scroll bars. A vertical scroll bar will let you move up or down, and a horizontal scroll bar will let you move side to side. In some apps, the scroll bars don't appear until you move your mouse toward the bottom or right side of the app window.

Each scroll bar has three parts:

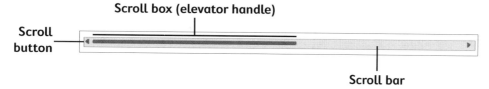

HANDS-ON 4.5 Use Scroll Bars

In this exercise, you will resize the Paint window and use the vertical and horizontal scroll bars.

Before You Begin: Resize the Paint window so scroll bars appear.

1. **Restore Down** ⬜ the Paint window. Click the edge of the program window until you see vertical and horizontal scroll bars.

2. Follow these steps to practice scrolling up and down:

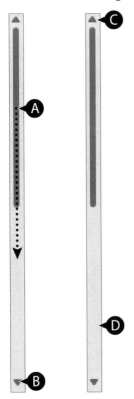

A Point at the scroll box, hold down the mouse button, and drag it downward about an inch.

B Click several times on the down scroll button to scroll down farther.

C Click several times on the up scroll button to scroll back to the top.

D Click once on the scroll bar to jump farther down than you would by scrolling with the down scroll button.

3. Try using parts of the horizontal scroll bar to scroll from side to side.

4. Close Paint. Do not save the file.

Typing with the Word Online App

Word for the web is a free and basic word-processing program from Microsoft that is used to type letters and other simple documents. Although it is a basic app, it makes an excellent learning program because it has many features common to other online and desktop applications.

Word Ribbon

Like the Paint program, Word uses a Ribbon instead of the traditional system of a menu bar and toolbars. Many of the features in Word's Ribbon are like those found in Microsoft Word 2016 and 2019.

Tabs

The Word Ribbon contains multiple tabs. On each tab, tools with a related function are assembled into command groups, which are further divided by vertical separators and labeled.

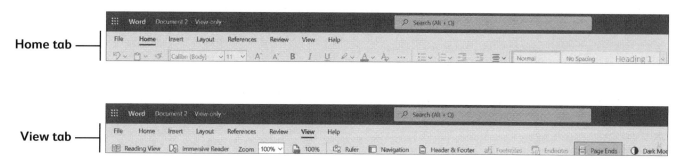

Home tab

View tab

Drop-Down Lists

Word has several drop-down lists on the Home tab that are represented and accessed by clicking a button containing a downward-pointing arrow. Three frequently used drop-down lists are located in the Font group: Font Name, Font Size, and Font Color. Some drop-down lists (such as Font Name) are quite long and include a scroll bar.

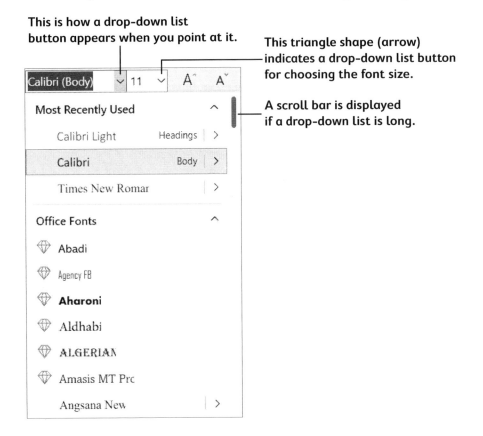

This is how a drop-down list button appears when you point at it.

This triangle shape (arrow) indicates a drop-down list button for choosing the font size.

A scroll bar is displayed if a drop-down list is long.

ScreenTips

Just as you saw in Paint, when you rest your mouse pointer over a tool or drop-down list in the Ribbon in Word, a ScreenTip helps you determine its name and function.

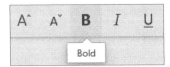

Tip! When you discover a useful feature such as ScreenTips in one program, check to see if the same feature is used in other programs.

Simplified Ribbon Mode

Word has the ability to switch from Ribbons back to traditional toolbars. Toolbars have fewer options and take up less room on the screen. The Simplified Ribbon option is located in the Ribbon Display Options menu at the right side of the Ribbon.

Example of a Ribbon with Simplified Ribbon mode enabled

The Cursor and the Mouse Pointer

Users who are new to word-processing programs such as Word can be confused by what appears to be two cursors: One is the blinking **cursor** in the text, and the other is the *mouse pointer* (which can appear almost everywhere you point). The blinking cursor is often also called the **insertion point**. When you type, the text is inserted to the left of the blinking cursor.

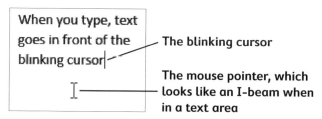

When Word is first opened, the blinking cursor is located at the top of the white writing area. This white writing area is equivalent to a sheet of paper.

Tip! Most of the word-processing skills learned in this chapter can be used to type email and work in most other word-processing programs.

Special Keys on the Keyboard

Computer keyboards have keys that perform tasks that are particular to working with apps. This section discusses some of the most popular ones, and in the next exercise, you'll use these keys and more.

Backspace and Delete Keys

The Backspace key on the keyboard erases text to the left of the cursor. The Delete key erases text to the right of the cursor.

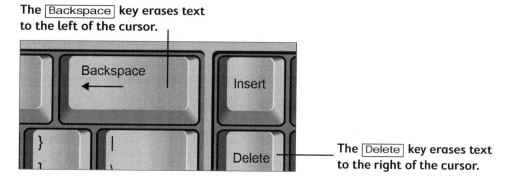

Tab Key

The Tab key moves the cursor right to the next half-inch mark on the ruler. This is a useful key for creating accurately aligned columns.

Enter Key

The ⌴Enter⌴ key has two functions: It ends a paragraph, and it moves any text below or to the right of the cursor down two lines. Holding the ⌴Shift⌴ key and tapping ⌴Enter⌴ moves the cursor down one line.

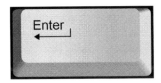

HANDS-ON 4.6 Type in the Word Online App

In this exercise, you will do basic typing using the ⌴Spacebar⌴ and ⌴Enter⌴ keys; correct mistakes using ⌴Backspace⌴ and ⌴Delete⌴; and move around using the ⌴Home⌴, ⌴End⌴, and arrow keys.

Before You Begin: Log in to OneDrive using the instructions from Chapter 3, "Creating an Online Account."

1. Click the **app launcher** on the left side of the OneDrive title bar and then click **Word** on the menu that appears.

2. Choose **New Blank Document**.

3. **Maximize** the browser window.

4. Type the following:

   To: ⌴Spacebar⌴**Emily**⌴Spacebar⌴**Carlito**⌴Shift⌴+⌴Enter⌴**From:** ⌴Spacebar⌴**Dan**⌴Spacebar⌴**Lewis**⌴Enter⌴**Dear**⌴Spacebar⌴**Emily,**

   Notice that using the ⌴Spacebar⌴ puts a space between words. When ⌴Shift⌴+⌴Enter⌴ is typed, it ends a paragraph and moves the cursor down one line. When the ⌴Enter⌴ key is typed by itself, it ends the paragraph and moves the cursor down two lines.

5. Tap ⌴Enter⌴ to create two new lines and then type the following:

   If I type a sentence that is too long to fit on one line, I do not have to tap the Enter key when I get near the margin because the words will automatically wrap to a new line.⌴Enter⌴
   Typing is fun.

   Most word-processing and email programs automatically wrap text. It is necessary to tap ⌴Enter⌴ only when you want to end a paragraph and force text to start on a new line.

6. Leave Word open.

Editing Text

Word processing enables you to extensively edit and format the text before it is printed. When you are typing text, concentrate on getting your ideas typed first and worry about spelling, grammar, and layout later.

Tip! When typing a letter, report, or story, you do not have to stop and make corrections as you type. You can always make corrections later. If you stop to correct errors, you break your train of thought and may forget some important ideas.

Selecting Text

Text is *selected* before it can be edited (changed). Selecting text lets the computer know which part of the text to change. When text is selected, it typically becomes highlighted as though it is marked with a highlighter pen.

Word highlights selected text.

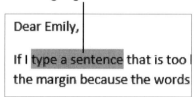

Dear Emily,

If I type a sentence that is too the margin because the words

There may be more than one way to select the same text, and you will become more productive if you become familiar with the different selection methods.

SELECTING TEXT	
Selection Procedure	**Result**
Drag with mouse	Selects a letter, word, sentence, or paragraph
Double-click	Selects a word
Triple-click	Selects an entire paragraph

Ctrl + A to select an entire document

🖱 HANDS-ON 4.7 Select Text

In this exercise, you will select text by dragging and clicking with the mouse.

Before You Begin: Word should still be open.

1. Follow these steps to select text:

Ⓐ Put the mouse pointer in front of the word *automatically*.

Ⓑ Drag to the end of the word and then release the mouse button. Word highlights the word you selected.

Ⓒ Click somewhere else to deselect (turn off) the highlighted word.

2. Place the mouse pointer over the word *automatically* and double-click.

   Word selects the entire word and the space after the word. This is a bit easier than dragging to select the single word.

3. Click away from the word to deselect it.

4. Drag the mouse pointer over the entire first paragraph to select it and then click away from it to deselect it.

5. Point the mouse pointer over the first paragraph and triple-click to select it; click away from it to deselect it.

   When you triple-click, you do not have to click rapidly. Just click three times smoothly without moving the mouse. Word selects the entire paragraph.

Save Your Work

When you finish a significant piece of work on a document, it's always a good idea to save it.

6. Choose **File→Save As**.

   Word displays the various save options.

7. Choose the **Save As** button to save a copy to OneDrive.

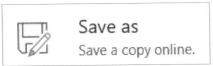

8. Select the **Documents** folder and then click the **Select** button to save in the default OneDrive location.

In Chapter 7, "Storing Files," you will learn more about creating folders for saving and organizing your files.

9. Type the new filename **Memo to Emily Carlito** and click **Save**.

Your document is now saved to OneDrive. Notice that the name of your document is now in the title bar for Word.

10. Leave Word open.

Formatting Text

Another editing task you can perform is text formatting. Formatting text in Word includes choosing a text style (Font Name), text size (Font Size, Grow Font Size, or Shrink Font Size), text attributes (**Bold**, *Italic*, <u>Underline</u>), and text color (Font Color). These button or drop-down list choices can be found on the Home tab in the Font group.

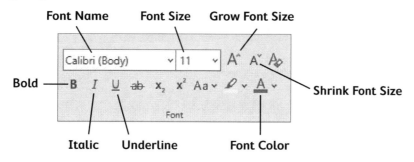

The Font group on the Home tab in Word

Note! Remember, you must select the text you want to format *before* you choose any formatting changes.

🖱 HANDS-ON 4.8 Format Text

In this exercise, you will change formatting using various buttons and drop-down lists.

Before You Begin: Word should still be open.

1. Follow these steps to make formatting changes to the text you have typed:

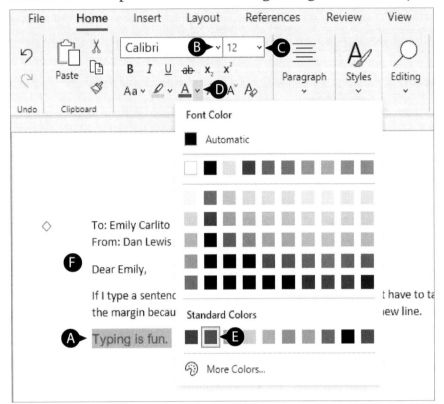

Ⓐ Drag or triple-click to select the last paragraph (make sure this text stays selected as you perform steps B–E).

Ⓑ Click the **Font Name menu** button ⌄ and choose **Calibri**.

Ⓒ Click the **Font Size menu** button ⌄ and choose **12**.

Ⓓ Click the **Font Color menu** button ⌄.

Ⓔ Choose any text color.

Ⓕ Click once on a clear area to deselect the text.

As you can see, as long as the text remains selected, you can repeatedly apply formatting commands to it.

2. Follow these steps to format a single word:

Ⓐ Double-click on the word **Carlito** to select it.

Ⓑ Change the style to **Bold**.

Ⓒ Change the color to **Blue**.

Ⓓ Click on a clear area to deselect the word.

It's easy to select and format single words.

3. Leave Word open.

Printing a Document

You may want to print a drawing or letter you have created. Most apps provide three commands to help you print:

- **Print Preview**—Preview the document on the monitor and make changes before you print.
- **Quick Print**—Send the document directly to the printer without any changes.
- **Print**—Select the printer, pages to print, number of copies, and other options before printing.

Print commands can be accessed on the File menu and sometimes via buttons on a toolbar.

Online Apps

Because of the way online apps are designed, your document has to be converted into a printable form. This is usually done by converting it into a PDF file (see Saving a File as a PDF) or some other format and displaying it in a separate printing window.

Word for the Web

Word creates a temporary PDF file that then can be printed using the print function of your browser. After you print, the browser tab is closed and the temporary PDF file is deleted.

Ctrl + P to start the print process in most apps

🖱 HANDS-ON 4.9 Print a Word Document

In this exercise, you will print the Memo to Emily Carlito.

Before You Begin: Word should still be open.

1. Choose **File→Print**.

2. Click the **Print** button.

3. In the dialog box that appears, click the **Print** button.
   When the printing is complete, the dialog boxes will close.

4. Leave Word open for the next exercise.

Saving as a PDF File

PDF is short for *portable document format*. PDF files store a document exactly as it was created, with all of its layout, text, and graphics intact.

PDF files are a popular way to share documents as they are machine and software independent, meaning that you don't need a specific piece of software or device to read the file. Many programs and devices can read PDF files, so the format has become a standard for sharing documents.

Many programs allow you to save your work as a PDF file. This is usually done in one of two ways: Printing to a PDF or using the Save As function to save as a PDF. Printing as a PDF means you print to a PDF "printer" instead of to your default printer.

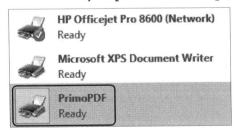

Example of a PDF "printer"

Instead of printing to paper, your document is saved to a PDF. During the process, you are given a chance to name the PDF file.

Some programs have you use the Save As function to save a copy of your document as a different file type.

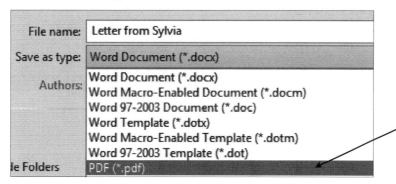

During the saving process, while naming the file, you can choose to save your document in PDF format. Online apps, like Word, may have slightly different ways for saving a document as a PDF.

HANDS-ON 4.10 Save a PDF File in Word

In this exercise, you will save a copy of your Memo to Emily Carlito as a PDF.

1. Choose **File→Save As**.

2. Click the **Download as PDF** button.

   Word converts a copy of your document into a temporary PDF file.

3. In the dialog box that appears, click the **Download** button.

   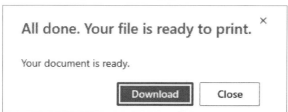

   The PDF is downloaded to the default download location for the Microsoft Edge browser. (More information on file locations and downloads can be found in later chapters.)

4. Leave Word open.

Cut, Copy, and Paste

Most Windows apps support the Cut, Copy, and Paste commands. In Word these commands are located in the Clipboard group on the Home tab.

CUT, COPY, AND PASTE COMMANDS	
Command	**Performs**
Cut	Deletes a selected object from its present location and places a copy of the object in a special folder called Clipboard.
Copy	Places a copy of a selected object in Clipboard without deleting it from its present location.
Paste	Inserts a copy of the last object cut or copied into the present location of the cursor.
Cut and Paste	Used together, they let you move text and other objects from one place in a program to another place within the same program (or to another program).
Copy and Paste	Used together, they let you copy text or another object from one place in a program to another place within the same program (or to another program).

Tip! In some apps you can move (cut and paste) selected text by dragging and dropping it to a new location. You can make a copy of text that has been selected to paste elsewhere by dragging and dropping the selected text to the new location while holding down the Ctrl key.

USING CUT OR COPY AND PASTE COMMANDS	
Task	**Procedure**
Use Cut or Copy and Paste	■ Select the text or object you want to move or copy. ■ Choose Home tab→Cut or Home tab→Copy. ■ Place the cursor where you want to paste the text or object. ■ Choose Home tab→Paste. ■ You can paste the text or object again by repeating the preceding two steps.

Keyboard Shortcuts

Some apps, especially browser-based apps, can't use the Cut, Copy, and Paste buttons because of design issues with the browser and the apps.

You will see a message like this when required to use keyboard shortcuts.

You can still cut, copy, and paste, but you will have to use the keyboard shortcuts.

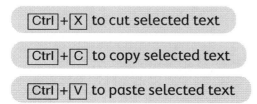

Advanced Cut, Copy, and Paste

The ability to copy objects from one program to another is a powerful tool. As your skills with the computer increase, you will find that you can copy more than just text from one app to another. For example, you can do the following:

- Copy text and images from the internet into your research paper (don't forget to cite your sources!)
- Copy a chart from a spreadsheet into a report or assignment
- Copy information from your notes into your presentation

The general rule to follow is if you can select an item, you can probably copy and paste it.

HANDS-ON 4.11 Use Cut and Paste

In this exercise, you will cut and paste text and move it within a Word document. Use keyboard shortcuts if needed.

Before You Begin: Word should still be open to your typed document from the last exercise. Also, make sure the Simplified Ribbon is turned off and the Classic Ribbon is turned on.

1. Follow these steps to move a paragraph using Cut and Paste:

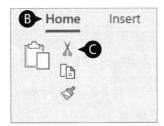

Ⓐ Drag or triple-click to select the last paragraph.

Ⓑ Click the **Home** tab.

Ⓒ Choose **Cut**.

Word cuts the text and places it in the Clipboard, and the text disappears from the document. Now that the text is in the Clipboard, you can paste it to a new location.

2. Click once at the end of the last sentence to place the blinking cursor there.

If I type a sentence that is too long to fit on one line, I do not have to tap the Enter key when I get near the margin because the words will automatically wrap to a new line.

Placing the cursor in the document tells Word where you want your next command (Paste) to be performed.

3. Choose **Home→Paste**.

Word pastes the text from the Clipboard back into the document.

4. Tap ⎡Enter⎤ and then choose **Home→Paste** from the Ribbon again.

Word pastes the text again. Whatever you cut or copy to the Clipboard remains there until you cut or copy something else, so you can paste the same item repeatedly if you wish.

> If I type a sentence that is too long to fit on one line, I do not have to tap the Enter key when I get near the margin because the words will automatically wrap to a new line. **Typing is fun.**
>
> **Typing is fun.**

5. Choose **Undo** from the Ribbon.

Undo

Word undoes your most recent command, which in this case is Paste.

6. Close the Microsoft Edge browser. Your work is saved automatically.

Closing the browser will close the Word tab.

- -

Self-Assessment

To check your knowledge of the key concepts introduced in this chapter, complete this Self-Assessment quiz.

1. Use the Cut and Paste commands to move selections from one place to another.   **true false**

2. A flash drive can be plugged into any USB port on a PC.   **true false**

3. When typing text, new text is inserted in front of the I-beam mouse pointer and not in front of the blinking cursor.   **true false**

4. Saving a file takes it from RAM and places a copy onto a drive.   **true false**

5. "My current letter-22" is a valid filename.   **true false**

6. The [Backspace] key moves the cursor to the left without erasing text.   **true false**

7. Which command reverses your most recent task?

    A. Undo

    B. Cut

    C. Paste

    D. Save

8. The feature on the side and bottom of a program window that enables you to view a large picture or file is the _____.

    A. elevator bar

    B. scroll bar

    C. zoom bar

    D. view bar

9. Before you save your work in a program for the first time, where is it being saved temporarily?

    A. On the hard drive

    B. On the USB flash drive

    C. In RAM

    D. In the monitor

10. Use the Save As command to _____.

    A. save a copy of a file to different location

    B. save a copy of a file with a different name

    C. save an unsaved file with a name and to a location of your choosing

    D. All of the above

⊕ Skill Builders

SKILL BUILDER 4.1 **Create and Save a Letter from Start to Finish**

In this exercise, you will create, edit, and format a letter for Sylvia to use in her goldfish aquarium business and save it to OneDrive.

1. Log in to OneDrive and start Word.

2. Open a new **Blank Document**.

3. Maximize the Microsoft Edge window.

4. Type this letter. You can use [Backspace] and [Delete] to correct errors as you type or wait until you are finished to select mistyped words and replace them.

   `Dear Business Owner,`[Enter]

   `Thank you for your interest in having an aquarium placed in your main lobby. I have enclosed a price list for the aquariums I have available. All prices include initial setup of the aquarium, the first group of goldfish, and appropriate aquatic plants.`[Enter]

   `Unless you have qualified staff to maintain the aquarium, I recommend our affordable monthly service. Our service is guaranteed.`[Enter]

   `I will arrange an appointment next week to review the details.`[Enter]

   `Sincerely,`[Enter]

   `Sylvia Tiger-Shark`[Shift]+[Enter]
   `Owner`[Shift]+[Enter]
   `Living Office`[Enter]

Edit the Letter

5. If you have not done so already, select any errors and replace them with corrected text.

6. Press [Ctrl]+[A] to select all text in the document.

7. Use the **Font Size** to change the font size to **12 pt**.

8. Click once somewhere in the document to deselect the text.

9. Select the words **Living Office** on the last line and make them **Bold**.

Save the Letter

10. Choose **File→Save As** and then click the **Save As** button.

11. In the OneDrive dialog box, click **Select** to save your file to the default location.

12. Type the filename `Letter from Sylvia` and click **Save**.

13. Leave Word open for the next exercise.

SKILL BUILDER 4.2 Create a Copy of Your Letter

In this exercise, you will create a copy of Letter from Sylvia from the last lesson and address it to a specific person.

1. In Word, choose **File→New**.

2. Open a **New Blank Document**.

3. Click on the browser tab for the **Letter from Sylvia**.

4. Press `Ctrl`+`A` to select the entire letter.

5. Press `Ctrl`+`C` to copy the letter to the Clipboard.

6. Click the browser tab named for the blank document you created.

7. Press `Ctrl`+`V` to paste the letter into the document.

8. Delete the text *Business Owner* and replace with: `Office Manager`

> Dear Office Manager,
>
> Thank you for your interest in havin
> for the aquariums I have available.
> goldfish, and appropriate aquatic pl

9. Save the file to the OneDrive default location as: `Office Manager Letter`

Save as a PDF

10. Choose **File→Save As** and then choose **Download as PDF**.

11. Click the **Download** button on the dialog box that appears.

12. Close Microsoft Edge.

CHAPTER 5

Using Email

LEARNING OBJECTIVES

- Create a properly formatted email address
- Send and receive emails, including those with attachments
- Create folders and organize emails using Outlook
- Identify spam and other email threats

In this chapter, you will learn about email and how email addresses are formatted. As you progress through the chapter, you will learn how to use the Outlook app to send, receive, and organize your email as well as to learn about security tips to protect against threats that come through email.

Learning Resources: **boostyourskills.lablearning.com**

Case Study: Time for Email

Jodi has a problem. She recently enrolled in college, and everyone wants her email address. Jodi wants to have a separate school email but doesn't know how to get one.

Jodi talks with her friend Nadia, who explains that she can get a free email address from Microsoft and then shows Jodi how to use Outlook to send and receive emails. Nadia also explains how Jodi can use any device, including her smartphone, to send and receive her new school emails. Before long, Jodi is spending as much time emailing on her laptop as she does talking on her phone!

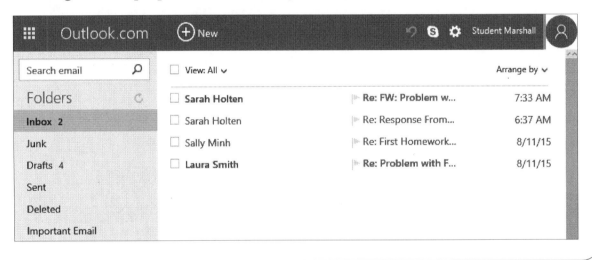

What Is Email?

Email was first created in 1971 when Ray Tomlinson, an early Internet pioneer, was tasked with finding something interesting to do with the earliest version of the Internet. Today, an estimated 300 billion emails are sent around the world every day.

Email is an electronic message that is sent over the Internet. A message can contain text, graphics, and more. Files, called attachments, can be connected to your email message, making it a fast and efficient way to send documents and photos.

How Does Email Work?

Email works like sending a letter through the U.S. Post Office. When you send an email, you use a person's individual email address, which points to a specific electronic post office, called an email server, on the Internet. When that person checks for email, their messages are copied from the email server onto their computer, device, or smartphone.

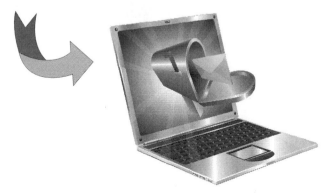

Email Address

Your email address is like your street or PO box address; it identifies the location where people can send messages to you. Your email address is unique, and you are the only one who can have that specific email address.

yourname@domain.com

An email address is made of two pieces: a local piece and a domain piece separated by an @ (pronounced "at") symbol. The local piece is your unique name, like an individual PO box number, and the domain piece after the @ symbol defines the location of your electronic post office on the Internet.

Note! The @ symbol was chosen because of all the nonalphanumeric characters on the keyboard that didn't already have a function, it was the least likely to be confused with being part of the local name.

The Outlook Online App

Outlook for the web, which used to be called Outlook.com, is a free, web-based email service that you can use to send, receive, and organize your emails. It's a basic version of the full version app, Microsoft Outlook, which, like the full version of Microsoft Word, is available for purchase.

The Outlook online app and the full version of Outlook are similar. You will find that many businesses use Outlook as their primary email program.

 Gmail **yahoo/mail**

Other free email services exist and are widely used on the Internet. Some of the most popular include Gmail, Yahoo! Mail, and Mail.com.

Logging in to Outlook is very similar to logging in to Word. Both use the same login that you created in Chapter 3, "Creating an Online Account."

HANDS-ON 5.1 Log In to Outlook

In this exercise, you will log in to Outlook for the first time. The first step is to log in to OneDrive.

1. Start Microsoft Edge.

2. Type **onedrive.live.com** into the address bar of the browser and press [Enter].

3. Sign in to OneDrive, if necessary.
    See Hands-On 3.3, steps 6–9, if you have any problems.

Log In to Outlook

4. Click the **app launcher** on the left side of the OneDrive title bar and then click **Outlook**.

5. Choose **Skip for Now** if it asks about adding an Outlook email address.
    Anytime Outlook asks if you want to create an email address, just skip or decline. Messages will pop up on a regular basis about creating an Outlook email address, but since you already have an email address associated with this account, you do not need to do so.

6. Close Outlook.

The Outlook Screen

The Outlook screen is very dynamic; the screen changes to show you the commands you need at that moment. Instead of a Ribbon with multiple tabs full of commands, the app provides a menu bar containing changing commands.

For example, when you are preparing to send a new email, the menu bar changes to show you only the relevant sending commands, and a formatting menu appears.

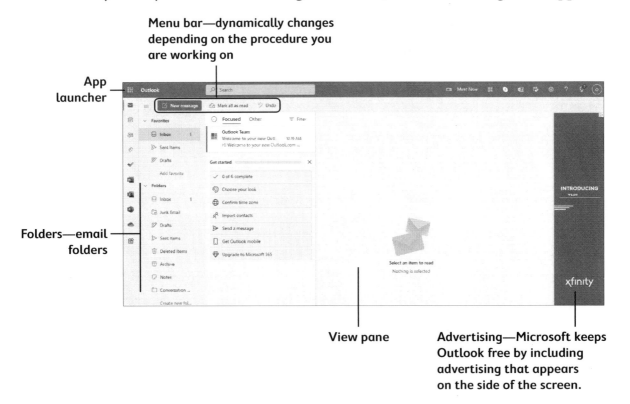

The Inbox shows some basic information about the emails that have been sent to you, including the name of the sender, the subject, and the date/time it was sent. It also shows the following icons, which contain commands relating to email:

When you use your mouse pointer to hover over the subject line of an email, you are shown commands for deleting it, marking it as read/unread, or keeping it on the top of the list of emails as a priority. You can also click an email's subject line to read it.

HANDS-ON 5.2 Read an Email

In this exercise, you will open and read an email from the Outlook Team.

Before You Begin: Log in to OneDrive using the instructions in Hands-On 3.3.

1. Click the **app launcher** on the left side of the OneDrive title bar and then click **Outlook** on the menu that appears.

2. Open the email from the Outlook Team by clicking on its subject line.

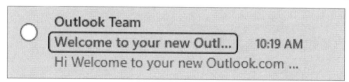

If you have a moment, read through the email and learn about some of the things Outlook can do.

3. Close Outlook.

. . . .

Sending Messages

One of the primary jobs of any email app is to facilitate the sending of messages. Starting an email message in Outlook is as simple as clicking the New Message button.

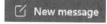

Messages include the following components:

- The recipient's email address
- A subject line (not required, but highly recommended)
- Message body text
- Attachments (optional)

Once the first three steps are completed (attaching a file is optional), your email is ready to be sent.

Message options displayed on a menu bar

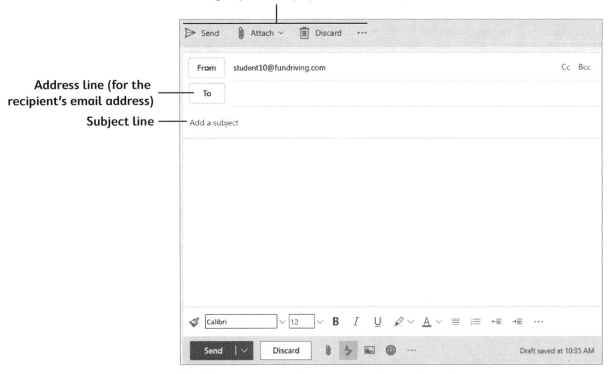

Address line (for the recipient's email address)

Subject line

Drafting a new email message—Outlook on the web

Message options are further condensed when using Outlook.com on a smartphone.

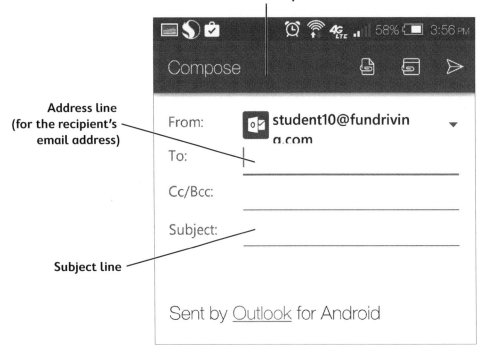

Address line (for the recipient's email address)

Subject line

Drafting a new email message—Android smartphone

Address Line

The address line (preceded by the word *To*) is where you enter a recipient's email address. It's very important to type the recipient's email address completely and exactly.

Multiple email addresses can be added by separating addresses with a comma.

Clicking the Cc (carbon copy) link located at the end of the address line tells the app to provide a new address line for entering other recipients who should receive a copy of the same email. Many times in business you cc someone on a message when you want to make that person aware of what is going on but don't require a response.

The Bcc (blind carbon copy) link works like carbon copy, except the recipient(s) of the email does not know that a different recipient is also receiving a copy.

An email address can be removed from a message by clicking the Close button to the right of the address.

MESSAGE ADDRESS OPTIONS	
Option	Description
To	The primary address line in an email
Cc, or carbon copy	Sends a copy of the email to another recipient
Bcc, or blind carbon copy	Sends a copy of the email to another recipient without the original recipient knowing
"," (comma)	Separates multiple email addresses in the address line

Subject Line

The subject line briefly describes the email's topic, and many people consider it to be as important as the message itself. This is because many office workers get hundreds of emails a day, and they use the subject lines to help them decide which emails to read first.

Keep the subject line very short and to the point.

SUBJECT LINE EXAMPLES	
Bad Subject Line	**Good Subject Line**
Homework	Homework assignment #4 attached
Approved	Changes to Project Approved
Need Help!	Need Help With Windows Problem

Writing Your Message

Writing your message works just like typing text in Word. Text can be formatted with bold, italics, and underline, and the color, font, and size of text can also be changed.

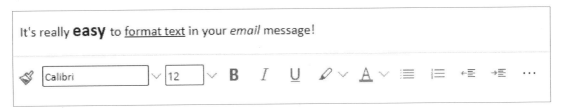

You may also copy and paste text from other apps directly into the email message. This is useful for sharing quotes or other information you have found on the Internet.

HANDS-ON 5.3 Send an Email Message

In this exercise, you will send an email message.

1. Open Outlook.

2. Click the **New Email** button on the menu bar.

3. In the address line type **laura.smith@lablearning.net** and then click the **Cc** link to open a carbon copy address line.

Notice a second address line opens.

4. In the Cc address line, type **dcampbell@lablearning.net** and click in the subject line.

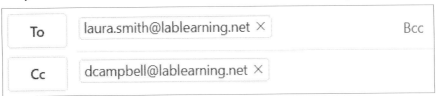

5. In the subject line type **Problem with Free Bobble-head Offer** and then click in the message area of the email.

6. Type the following in the message area:

To Whom It May Concern, `Enter`
`Enter`
I recently registered on your website to receive a free collectible bobble-head doll. It has been six weeks, and I have not received any reply or the free doll. `Enter`
`Enter`
If possible, please let me know the status of my doll. `Enter`
`Enter`
Thank you, `Enter`

7. Type your name.

8. Click the **Send** button below the message.

   Your message is immediately sent, a copy is moved to the Sent folder, and you are returned to the Inbox.

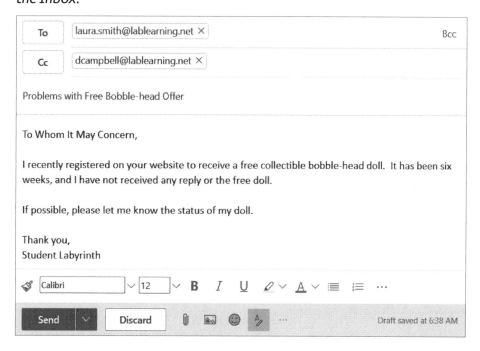

9. Close Outlook.

· ·

Attachments

Emails can have files attached that are sent with the message. You can attach almost any file type, including documents, images, recordings, and videos.

Depending on the company providing the email service, there may be limits on the types of files allowed in attachments. For example, many email providers do not let you send apps as attachments due to the security risks.

Email providers may also limit the size of the email attachments you send. This size maximum varies depending on the provider. For example, Gmail and Outlook both limit the size of attachments to 25 megabytes.

Tip! Even if your email provider does not limit the size of attachments, your recipient's provider may, which may mean that they won't be able to open a large attachment that you send or that the message may not be delivered.

HANDS-ON 5.4 Send an Email with an Attachment

In this exercise, you will send a file that you created in Chapter 4, "Working with Apps," as an email attachment.

Before You Begin: This exercise assumes you saved the My Signature file you created in Hands-On 4.3 on your USB flash drive.

1. Open Outlook.

2. Click the **New Mail** button on the Outlook menu bar.

3. In the address line type: `instructorsally@gmail.com`

4. In the subject line type: `First Homework Assignment`

5. Type the following in the message area:

   `Attached you will find homework assignment #1. Hopefully my drawing skills are up to your expectations!` `Enter` `Enter`
   `Thank you,` `Enter` `Enter`

6. Type your name.

7. Click **Attach** on the menu bar and then click **Browse This Computer** from the drop-down menu.

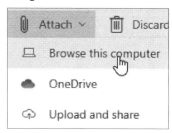

An Open dialog box will appear that will allow you to navigate to the location of the file you wish to attach.

8. Choose your USB flash drive from the Navigation pane on the left and then choose the **My Signature** file from the View pane on the right.

If in Hands-On 4.3 you saved your file to a different location, choose that location from the Navigation pane.

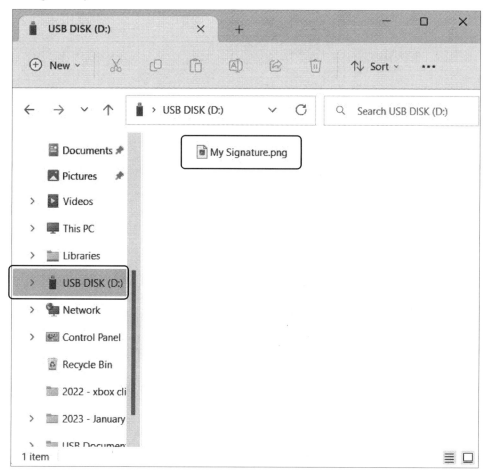

Remember that your USB flash drive may have a different name than what is shown here.

9. Click **Send** and then close Outlook.

Receiving and Replying to Messages

Outlook checks for messages every thirty minutes and displays those messages in your Inbox. By default, messages are displayed from newest to oldest, but you can change that sort order if desired.

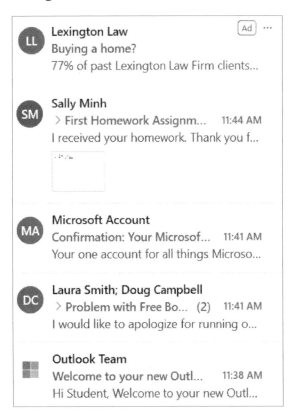

Messages that are unread will be in boldface type. Once you have opened a message, you have multiple options for handling it.

Replying

Replying enables you to quickly send a message back to the sender of an email. The Reply button enables you to reply to a message in three different ways:

TYPES OF REPLIES	
Reply Type	**What It Does**
Reply	Replies only to the original sender of the email
Reply all	Replies to everyone who received the email
Forward	Enables you to forward a copy of the email to a new recipient, choosing to include or not include the original sender

🖱 HANDS-ON 5.5 **Reply to an Email**

In this exercise, you will reply to an email sent to you.

Before You Begin: Have a friend or family member send you an email. The content is not important.

1. Open Outlook.

2. Click on the email you will reply to.

   If the email is not in the Focused section, click Other to find it there.

3. Click the **Reply** button at the bottom of the email.

   Notice that a blank email appears with the address line already populated and a copy of the previous message at the bottom of the email. Also notice that "RE:" has been added to the beginning of the subject line to indicate that you are replying to the original email.

4. Click next to the address and then click **Cc** and type:

   sholten@lablearning.net

   This will send a copy of the mail to Sarah Holten.

5. Type a short reply message and click **Send**.

6. Close Outlook.

· ·

Deleting

If you don't need an email anymore, you can delete it. Deleted email is moved to the Deleted folder and is permanently removed after ten days. Once removed, you cannot get it back.

When viewing an email, if you want to delete it, you can use the Delete button on the menu bar.

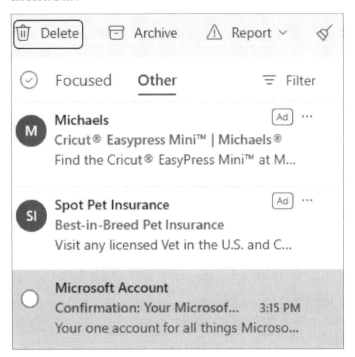

Saving Emails

The Inbox should not be used for saving emails. Doing this makes it difficult to see the new and recent emails you have to deal with as well as to find a specific email. Instead of storing emails in the Inbox, create folders.

Creating and Deleting Folders

Outlook enables you to create folders for sorting emails. Folders you create will appear on the Folders list on the left side of the screen along with the premade Outlook folders.

You can create folders for various activities like school, for a specific project, or even for specific timeframes like the quarters of the school year. The more organized your email is, the more efficient you will be at using it.

You can also delete folders that are no longer needed. When deleting a folder, you will get a warning message that any email in the folder will be deleted.

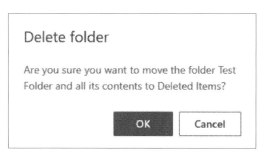

HANDS-ON 5.6 Create an Email Folder

In this exercise, you will create a folder for storing your important emails.

1. Start Outlook.

2. Click the **Create New Folder** command at the bottom of the Folders list.

3. Type **Important Email** and tap [Enter].

The folder Important Email *appears above the New Folder command.*

4. Create another folder called: **Research**

Delete a Folder

5. Right-click the **Research** folder and choose **Delete Folder** from the menu.

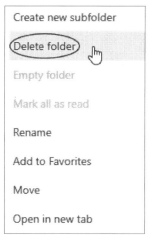

6. Click **OK** on the warning message that appears.

Note that any messages in the folder will be permanently deleted along with the folder.

7. Close Outlook.

Moving Emails

Outlook enables you to move emails to different folders in multiple ways. You can drag emails from the Inbox into the appropriate folder (the **drag-and-drop** method) or click in the check box to the left of the sender's name and use the Move To command. Each method accomplishes the same goal; use whichever method you prefer.

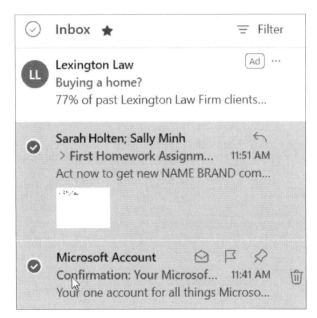

To move multiple files at one time, click the check box for each email and then execute the move.

HANDS-ON 5.7 Move Emails

In this exercise, you will move emails to the Important Email folder using both the Move To method and the drag-and-drop method.

1. Open Outlook.

2. Hover over the Outlook Team message to make a radio button appear; click the radio button to select the message.

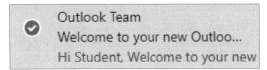

3. On the menu bar, click **Move To→Important Email.**

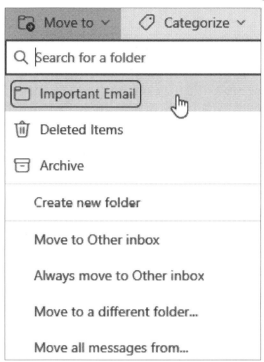

All the folders in the Folder list are listed on the Move To menu when you click the menu item.

4. Click the **Important Email** folder in the Folder list and verify that your email is there.

Drag Emails to Folders

5. Click the **Inbox** folder.

6. Drag the email from Laura Smith/Douglas Campbell over to the **Important Email** folder and release.

7. Click the **Important Email** folder and verify that the message is there.

8. Close Outlook.

Saving Email Addresses

Outlook enables you to save email addresses so you don't have to retype them over and over again. These frequently used addresses appear under the To line when you create a new email.

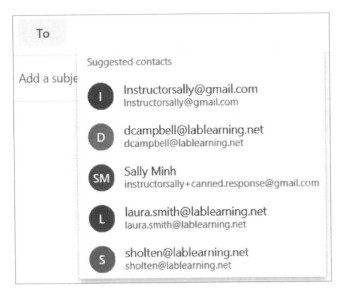

As you type an email address into the address line, the frequent contacts are filtered. When you see the address you want, you can click on it to add it to the address line.

Occasionally, Outlook will ask if you want to save a particular email address from an email that you have received. These messages will appear along the bottom of the Outlook window.

Email Safety

In a study done by IT security company Kaspersky Labs in the first quarter of 2013, they found that 70% of all email was unsolicited commercial email (spam) and that 2.4% of it had malicious attachments! Luckily, most problematic emails get filtered out before they reach your inbox.

Email represents one of the top ways your computer and devices are compromised, and the result can be machines that don't work, stolen information, compromised passwords, and wasted time.

With a few simple steps and a little bit of knowledge, you can dramatically reduce the threat malicious email poses to you.

Tip! Email is not secure. You should never send passwords, credit card numbers, personal information, or other sensitive information in an email message.

Understanding the Threats

What are the threats? There are four categories of malicious email activity: spam, phishing scams, advance fee scams, and spoofing.

Spam

Spam is as much a waste of time and resources as it is a threat. According to the US government, spam is unsolicited commercial email. Spam tries to sell products that may or may not be real in hopes of getting your credit card number and money. Once a scammer has your credit card number, you may or may not get the product.

Phishing

Phishing (pronounced like fishing) scams are focused on getting credit card numbers, logins, passwords, and other personal information like Social Security numbers. Generally, the emails look like they are from a bank, the government, cable companies, or other big entities that you may do business with. The emails look "real," as they usually have company logos and addresses in them, but any Internet links they contain don't really go to the company. Remember…no government agency or business will *ever* ask you for your credit card number, login, password, or Social Security number via email. EVER.

The following is an example of a Bank of America phishing email. It looks real but is completely phony. You can tell it is phony because Bank of America will never have you click links in an email; it will have you go to the bank site and log in. It would also never have the most obvious link on the page be the one for declining a service.

Finally, if you look closely at the message, you will see some spelling and grammatical errors, which a large company would not permit in important communications.

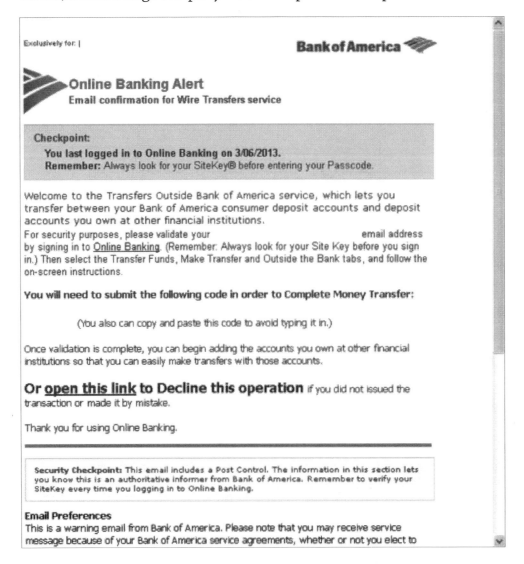

Spoofing

Spoofing is when someone forges an email address and sender name that makes the email look legitimate when it's not. Spoofing is often used as a part of other scams.

Advance Fee

Advance fee emails and scams try to get you to send money with the promise of great riches or deals. This scam plays on people's greed and/or desperation. In one form of this scam, a foreign person asks for your help because they have just inherited millions of dollars or have access to millions. They promise to share the money with you if you will advance them some funds to help move the inheritance to the United States.

```
RE: MR. RANDY CODY,
INVESTMENT MANAGER
PRIVATE & VERY SAFE
TONBRIDGE,
KENT TN11 9DZ,
UNITED KINGDOM .



I wish to inform you that this letter is not a hoax mail and I urge you to treat it serious. We want to transfer The
52,000,000.00 (Fifty Two Million
GBP) to any safe account with your honest assistance. I have every possibility for the accumulated proceed to be
paid in your favour and then both of us will share the value equal percentage Can I trust you on this?


Although, necessary steps has been made regards to this issue confidentially with key Bank Personnel?s and they have
agreed to help if I found honest and capable person to handle this transaction to enable us transfer the value Asset
out from UK.

I guarantee that this will be executed under a concrete special arrangement that will protect us from any breach of
law. I will not fail to bring to your notice that this transaction is total hitch-free and you should not entertain
any fear because good arrangement has been outlined for successful conclusion.

If you are willing and capable to handle this business with me in full confidence & trust, please do not hesitate to
Reply me back


I look forward hearing from you.

Warmest Regards.

MR. RANDY CODY,
```

An example of an advance fee scam email. If you were to respond to this email, eventually they would email you and ask for money.

Unfortunately, many people fall for these types of scams every year.

SPOTTING A MALICIOUS EMAIL	
Sign	Why is it a sign?
Bad grammar and misspellings	No company will send an email that contains spelling errors. Many malicious emails come from Africa, Russia, and Eastern Europe, where English is a second language.
It's too good to be true	This old saying applies to emails. If the deal is really good…it's probably an unsafe email.
Strange email from a friend	If you receive an email from a friend telling you to open the attachment or click on a link, or the message is not expected, contains only a link, and isn't personalized…it's probably an unsafe email.

(cont.)

SPOTTING A MALICIOUS EMAIL (cont.)	
Sign	Why is it a sign?
Personal email from someone you don't know	When someone's email or social media account is compromised, the email addresses of all their contacts are frequently spammed. For example, seniors may get emails from "grandkids" needing money to get out of a bind.
Unsolicited emails from the government or a private company	These emails may ask for your credit card numbers, login information, or Social Security number to "update your account," but government agencies and legitimate companies will always tell you to go directly to their site rather than requesting information in an email or having you follow a link.
The sender's email address has a domain that's a random series of characters	No legitimate company will have an email address that ends in something nonsensical, such as @2we34fgt.com.

Protecting Yourself

If you have read this far, you have done more to protect yourself than most people. Knowing what the threat looks like is half the battle.

Take the next steps to deal with spam and other malicious emails:

- Delete suspect emails—If you suspect that an email is spam or malicious, don't view it, click any links, or download any attachments. Doing so can trigger malicious actions attached to the email, such as installing a computer virus on your computer.
- Don't reply to spam—Replying to spam email lets the sender know that your email address is active and will increase the amount of spam you receive.
- Don't give out your email address—Limit who gets your email address. When signing up for free sites on the Internet, decide if it's really worth the spam you are going to get just to play a free game or activity.

Deleting Spam in Outlook

Besides automatically deleting known spam emails, Outlook gives you a way to remove spam that you receive.

Using the Report→Report Junk command on the menu bar moves the selected email to the Junk Email folder and marks the sender as unsafe. Email in the Junk Email folder is deleted after ten days.

HANDS-ON 5.8 Remove a Spam Message

In this exercise, you will remove a spam email using the Report Junk command.

1. Start Outlook.

2. Click the email from Sarah Holten.

   Notice that it has all the signs of a spam email—it's just way too good to be true.

3. Click the **Report** command on the menu bar and then select **Report Junk** from the menu.

   You are now viewing the next email from your Inbox. Sarah's email has been moved to the Junk Email folder.

4. Click the **Junk Email** folder.

   Notice that Sarah's email is in there. It will automatically be deleted in ten days.

5. Click the **Inbox** folder.

6. Close Outlook.

Self-Assessment

To check your knowledge of the key concepts introduced in this chapter, complete this Self-Assessment quiz.

1. An email address is made up of a local piece and a domain piece separated by an @ symbol.   **true   false**

2. Outlook is the only free email app available on the Internet.   **true   false**

3. You can send an email to only one recipient at a time.   **true   false**

4. You can attach documents only to your emails.   **true   false**

5. Outlook blocks much of the spam that is sent to you.   **true   false**

6. Multiple emails can be moved to a folder at the same time.   **true   false**

7. Which of these is NOT an Address line option?
   A. To
   B. Bcc
   C. Cc
   D. Tcc

8. Which of these is NOT an email threat?
   A. Spoofing
   B. Advance fee
   C. Phishing
   D. Sponging

9. The Move To command lets you _____.
   A. move selected emails to folders in Outlook
   B. move selected emails to folders on your computer
   C. move selected emails to OneDrive
   D. All of the above

10. Which of these is a potential sign of a malicious email?
    A. Bad grammar and misspellings
    B. Offer is too good to be true
    C. An email address with a domain containing a random series of characters
    D. All of the above

🏋 Skill Builders

SKILL BUILDER 5.1 Save Files from Links

In this exercise, you will save some images to your USB drive that were sent to you as links. These files will be used in later chapters.

1. Open Outlook.

2. Click the message from Sally Minh.

3. If you receive a warning that some parts of the message have been blocked, click the **Show Content** link.

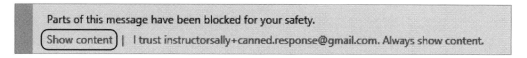

4. Click the link for **image1.png**.

    The image will be brought up in a new browser tab.

5. Click the **Download** button on the top-right corner of the screen.

    The image is downloaded to the Downloads folder.

6. Close the browser tab for image1.

7. Repeat steps 4–6 for the remaining three images.

8. Close Outlook.

SKILL BUILDER 5.2 Create a Gmail Email Account

There are many free email clients available. In this exercise, you will create a free Gmail email account. The process used to create other email accounts is likely to have some similar steps.

1. Start Microsoft Edge.

2. In the address bar type **mail.google.com** and click ⎡Enter⎤.

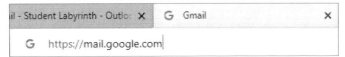

3. Click the **Create an Account** button and choose the **For Myself** option on the drop-down menu, if necessary.

4. Enter the information requested in the form. Choose a Gmail email address and password. When asked for your existing email address, use the same one that you used when creating your Microsoft account.

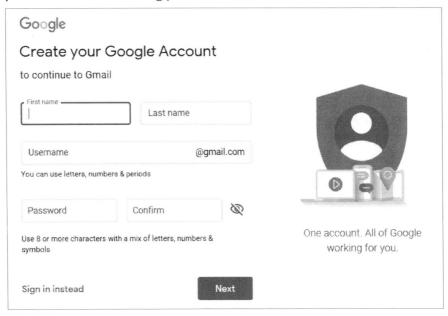

Make sure to write down your new Gmail address and login.

5. Enter your birth date and gender (optionally, you can enter a recovery phone number and/or email address) and then click the **Next** button.

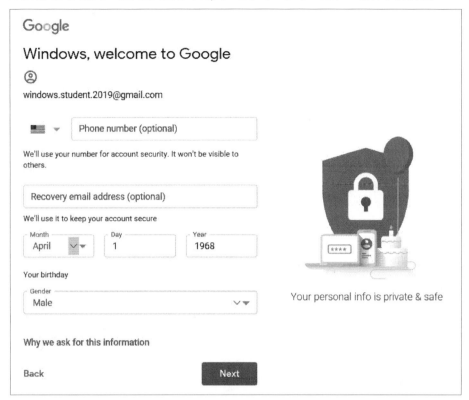

6. Scroll to the bottom of the terms of service and click the **I Agree** button.

7. Close the Get Started with Gmail screen.

8. Close your browser.

. . . .

SKILL BUILDER 5.3 Send and Read Email in Gmail

In this exercise, you will complete basic email procedures using Gmail.

1. Open Microsoft Edge and go to: **mail.google.com**

2. Click the **Compose** button on the left side of the screen.
   This brings up a New Message dialog box, similar to the one seen in Outlook.

3. Type the following message:

To: **laura.smith@lablearning.net**

Subject: **Crushed Bobble-Head**

To Whom It May Concern, Enter
Enter
**I just received my bobble-head doll, and it was crushed.
The shipping package was in good shape, so it looks like
it was damaged at the warehouse and shipped to me.** Enter
Enter
**I would like to know if a new bobble-head doll could be
shipped to me.** Enter
Enter
Thank you, Enter
Your Name

4. Click **Send** on the lower-left corner of the email.

   Your message is sent and a confirmation appears on the screen.

5. When the email appears, click on the subject line of the email **Crushed
   Bobble-Head**.

   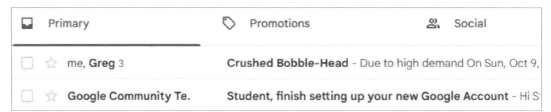

   *Notice the full email appears in Gmail with an area for you to Reply or Forward
   the email.*

6. Click the right arrow button on the upper-right corner of Gmail to read the next
   email.

   *Notice that Gmail shows the next email and that the Next button is now active. The back
   button allows you to go back to the previous email.*

7. Click the **Back to Inbox** button.

SKILL BUILDER 5.4 Delete and Archive Emails in Gmail

In this exercise, you will delete and archive emails in your Gmail account. To archive a message means to store it in a different folder. The message will not clutter your Inbox, but it's also not deleted, so if you need it again later, you can easily retrieve it.

1. Click the check box next to one of the emails from the Gmail Team.

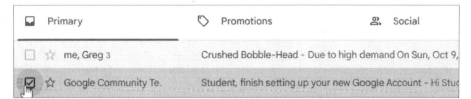

This selects the email. Multiple emails can be selected by clicking the check boxes next to them.

2. Click the **Delete** (trash can) button at the top of the email.

The selected email is sent to the Trash, and a confirmation appears at the bottom left of the Gmail window. Emails in the trash are permanently deleted after thirty days.

> Conversation moved to Trash.   Undo   ✕

3. Select the **Problems with Bobble-Head Offer** email.

If the email doesn't appear quickly, refresh your browser to force Gmail to retrieve it.

4. Click the **Archive** button at the end of the subject line.

The email is archived and can be accessed later if needed.

5. Close Microsoft Edge.

. . . .

SKILL BUILDER 5.5 Forward an Email

In this exercise, you will forward an email to a new recipient.

1. Open Outlook.

2. Click the email from Laura Smith/Douglas Campbell located in the Important Email folder.

3. Choose **Forward**.

4. Type **sholten@lablearning.net** in the To line.

   Notice that the Subject line already has been filled out and starts with Fw:, *which notifies the recipient that the email is a copy being forwarded.*

5. In the message area type: **It is great to see a company take responsibility for a mistake. I hope they can find me a bobble-head doll.**

   Notice that a copy of the original message has already been added.

6. Click **Send**.

7. Close Outlook.

UNIT 2: FILE MANAGEMENT

In this unit, you will explore ways to manage and organize files using Windows 11. Topics covered in Chapter 6 include the different types of storage media available for your use as well as how to use File Explorer to navigate and search for folders and files. In Chapter 7, you will explore how to create, move, copy, delete, and restore folders and files, and you will also learn about and use Microsoft's OneDrive file storage.

CHAPTER 6

Finding Files

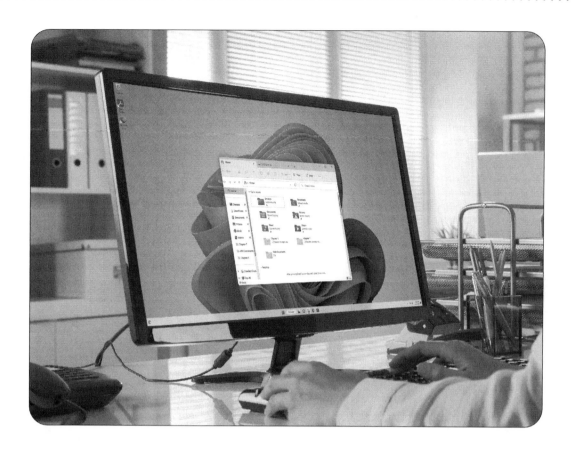

CHAPTER OBJECTIVES

- Describe and use various storage devices
- Use File Explorer to locate files and folders
- Plug in a USB flash drive
- Identify different types of folders used by Windows
- Find files and folders with File Search

Finding your files when you need them is obviously important. In this chapter, you will learn where to find a file you have created. You will also learn how files, folders, and drives are organized on your computer so you can navigate through the system. Finally, you will become familiar with the search tools in Windows that can help you find files that have been misplaced.

Learning Resources: **boostyourskills.lablearning.com**

📂 Case Study: Checking Up on the Hard Drive

Jamal has had his computer for a while, and he is growing concerned about two potential problems:

- Since he has a digital camera, he thinks the pictures he has been saving on his computer may fill the hard drive to its maximum capacity.

- He also worries that all of his files would be lost if he were to have a fire in his house or if the hard drive in his computer were to fail.

A friend suggests that Jamal could save backup copies of the files on one or more external hard drives. Because an external hard drive is portable, he could keep it in his desk at work. The external hard drive at work would keep the backup copies of his files safe from disasters at home.

Jamal first decides to determine the capacity of his hard drive and how much of it is being used. His friend shows him how to determine the capacity of the hard drive by looking at its Properties box. It looks like this:

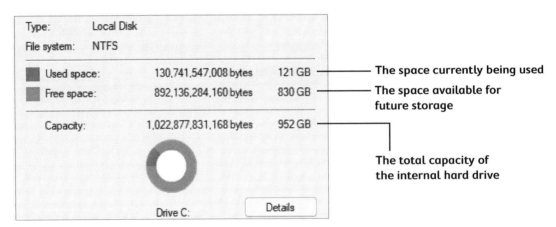

Jamal sees that the drive is not very full, so he decides to buy an external hard drive with a capacity of at least 1 TB and start backing up his files on the new drive on a regular basis.

About Storage Media

On most computers, you have many options for saving files you have created. Some of these storage devices are internal (inside the computer) and can't be moved. Others are portable and can be moved from computer to computer.

Types of Storage Devices

All of these devices can be used to store the various types of files you create, including documents, pictures, music, and videos.

Internal Hard Drive

This is the *permanent* storage inside the computer. Most of your files and all of the apps that run on your computer reside on this internal drive.

CD/DVD Drives

You can save files and folders on CDs or DVDs, and these are just like the ones your music and movies are saved on when you purchase them from a store. CDs and DVDs are used to store files because of their large storage capacity and their portability.

External Hard Drives

You can purchase hard drives that plug into your computer through a USB port (drives are discussed in the Behind the Screen: Drive Designations section). These external drives work just like internal hard drives, with the added advantage of being portable, enabling you to access your files from multiple computers.

USB Flash Drives

USB flash drives are sometimes referred to as keychain drives or thumb drives, and they are a type of removable storage. These small, key-sized drives allow you to easily carry files between computers at home, work, or anywhere.

You may have already used a USB flash drive to save your files in earlier chapters of this book. This chapter will provide you with more tips on using your USB flash drive.

Network Drives

Sometimes your computer will be connected to hard drives on other computers via a network. Although network drives may be located in another room or building, these remote drives can be used just like an internal drive or a portable storage device plugged into a USB port.

Viewing Storage Drives

In an office, you might store your paper files in a filing cabinet. The filing cabinet could have one drawer or many drawers. Storage on your computer is similar. Each storage device is like a drawer in a filing cabinet. Most desktop computers have two or more drives included: an internal hard drive and possibly a CD/DVD burner. Many laptops running Windows 11 do not have a CD/DVD burner. If you attach a USB flash drive to your computer, it is like having another drawer in which you can store data. Computers attached to a network may have access to even more drives.

Drive Letters

Windows provides an orderly process for dealing with multiple drives. Each drive is assigned a **drive letter** to help identify it. Obviously, you need to be able to view the drives and their drive letters, as well as the data stored on the drives, for them to be useful. File Explorer is the Windows feature that lets you view the drives and their data. (File Explorer is covered in more detail later in this chapter.)

Viewing the Drives

The Computer window lets you view the drives and then open the drives to see the data stored on them. In the following illustration, notice that File Explorer has grouped together the hard disk drives and the devices with removable storage. It also has displayed the drive names, drive letters, and information about each drive's capacity.

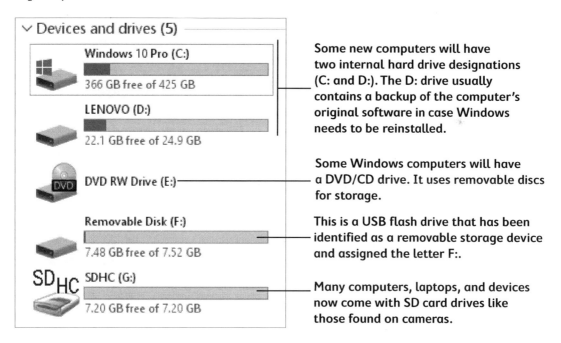

∨ Devices and drives (5)

Windows 10 Pro (C:)
366 GB free of 425 GB

Some new computers will have two internal hard drive designations (C: and D:). The D: drive usually contains a backup of the computer's original software in case Windows needs to be reinstalled.

LENOVO (D:)
22.1 GB free of 24.9 GB

DVD RW Drive (E:)

Some Windows computers will have a DVD/CD drive. It uses removable discs for storage.

Removable Disk (F:)
7.48 GB free of 7.52 GB

This is a USB flash drive that has been identified as a removable storage device and assigned the letter F:.

SDHC (G:)
7.20 GB free of 7.20 GB

Many computers, laptops, and devices now come with SD card drives like those found on cameras.

Drive Designations

Storage devices or drives in the computer are designated with letters of the alphabet followed by a colon (:). The alphabet letter and colon combination has been around since the early beginnings of computers, when there were no graphic images to represent drives.

What Determines Drive Order?

Numerous drives can be connected to your computer, and there are logical reasons why drives are assigned certain letters—at least for the first few drives in your computer.

Drive designations A: and B: are reserved for **floppy disk** drives. For years, this was the most common portable storage device. Computers sold now do not come with floppy drives; USB flash drives and SD card readers have replaced them. The C: drive is always the main internal drive in the computer. This is the drive on which the Windows software resides.

After the first three drive designations, the rules change a bit. You will see drives in various combinations and orders depending on how the computer is configured. Internal drives get designated first, starting with hard drives, followed by CDs and DVDs. Network drives are assigned next. External drives are last and are generally assigned designations based on the order in which they are attached to the computer.

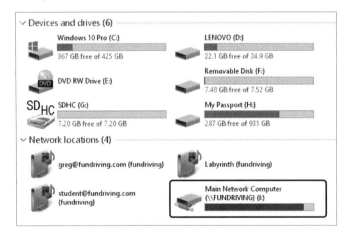

An example of a computer with six drives connected and four network drive connections. A red bar means that drive is really full! (Note: This screen is from a computer running an older version of Windows.)

Tip! Two important things to remember about drive letter assignments: 1) The main internal drive in the computer will always be drive C: and 2) your USB flash drive *will not necessarily have the same letter designation* on every computer with which it is used.

HANDS-ON 6.1 View Drives on Your Computer

In this exercise, you will view the various drives on your computer.

1. Click the **File Explorer** icon on the taskbar.

The File Explorer window appears.

2. Click **This PC** on the left side of the screen. Look at all the devices and drives listed on the right side of the screen.
   You may have to scroll down to find This PC.

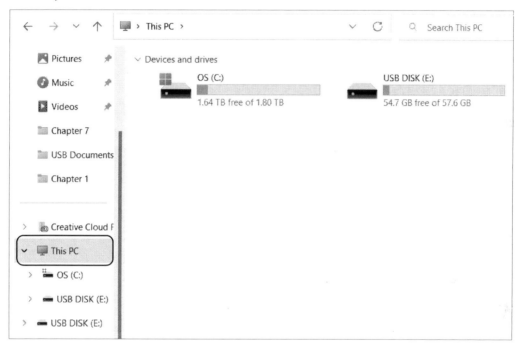

3. Close the File Explorer window.

· ·

Plugging In and Unplugging a Flash Drive

There is more to using a USB flash drive than simply inserting and removing it from a USB port on your computer. Your USB flash drive must be recognized by Windows when it is first plugged in and safely unplugged to avoid damage to data stored on the drive.

Plugging In

Your USB flash drive can be plugged into any USB port on a computer, but before you can use it, Windows must recognize the drive. Recognition can take a few moments.

Unplugging Safely

Before you remove your USB flash drive, you must make sure Windows is no longer using the drive for any reason, such as saving a file. There is a risk of damaging the files on the USB flash drive if it is unplugged improperly. If a USB flash drive has a blinking activity light or you're still using a file located on the drive, do not unplug the drive. Close any files located on the drive and wait for the light to stop blinking.

HANDS-ON 6.2 View Your USB Flash Drive

In this exercise, you will properly plug in your USB flash drive to the computer, open and close a file, and then safely unplug the flash drive.

1. If necessary, click the **File Explorer** icon on the taskbar.

2. Insert your USB flash drive into an available USB port on the computer and click **This PC** in the Navigation pane of File Explorer.

   Once your drive is recognized, it will show up in the File Explorer window under the Devices and Drives section, as shown in the following illustration. At this point, the USB flash drive is recognized and can be used like any other storage device on the computer. Take note of the name and drive letter because you will use these later in the exercise.

3. Close the AutoPlay window if it appears.

4. Double-click to open your USB flash drive.

   Windows displays the contents of the drive. If you used this drive in Chapter 4, "Working with Apps," you should see the documents and Paint pictures you created in that lesson.

5. Once the light on the USB flash drive has stopped blinking, you can safely unplug the drive from the computer.

6. Close File Explorer.

File Explorer

File Explorer (or simply Explorer) lets you view a computer's drives and the data on them. The following figure displays some of the key features of an Explorer window.

The address bar shows where you are in the drive and folder system. It also lets you move around in the drive and folder system.

The Search box allows you to look for files and folders.

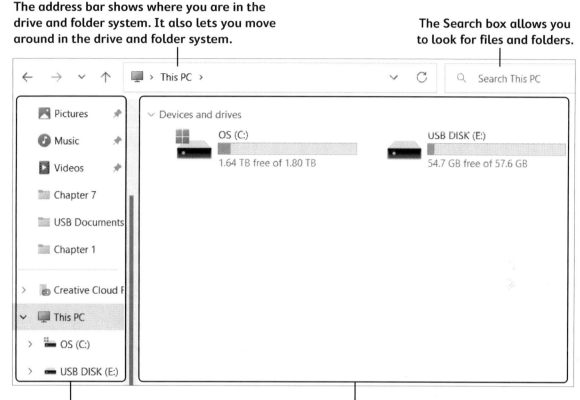

The Folders pane lets you view all folders on all drives.

The View pane shows you everything in the selected drive or folder. Here, since This PC is selected, we're seeing all drives.

Note! Throughout the rest of this book, the File Explorer window will be referred to as a folder window.

Common Folder Window Tasks

The folder window allows you to perform a number of useful tasks:

- **Browsing** for files and folders
- **Searching** for files and folders
- **Creating** new folders and using them to organize your documents
- **Renaming** files and folders
- **Moving and copying** files and folders
- **Deleting** files and folders

This chapter concentrates on the first two tasks—browsing and searching. The other tasks will be covered in Chapter 7, "Storing Files."

Locating Folders

When a new login name is created, Windows creates a set of folders on the internal hard drive. These folders are intended to be the storage locations for that individual's folders and files. Because of their importance as a person's primary storage locations, Windows also provides quick access commands to these folders from various locations, such as the Start menu and folder windows.

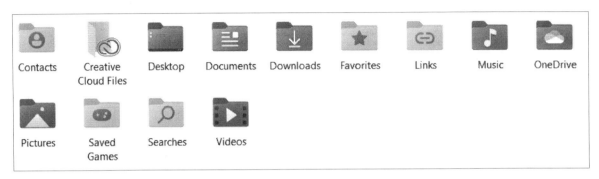

Tip! You can distinguish these folders from normal folders because they have custom graphics.

Navigating Your Drives and Folders

Being able to navigate drives and folders to locate your files is a critical skill. There are three easy-to-use navigation features built into the folder window:

- Address bar
- Folders pane
- Back and Forward buttons

Folders and Subfolders

Files are organized using folders. Folders can be further organized by adding more folders within them called **subfolders**. Any folder can have subfolders. This system is like having a filing cabinet drawer full of files organized into folders.

The Photos folder has a subfolder called *February*.
The February folder also has a subfolder called *Best*.

The Address Bar

The address bar runs across the top of a folder window and displays a **path** (hierarchy) that includes a starting location and any drive, folders, or subfolders linked to the location that are currently open. The path is like a map with signs pointing to your present location, and it is File Explorer's way of saying, "You are here, and this is how you got here." You can see how to navigate to your present location by following the path toward the left.

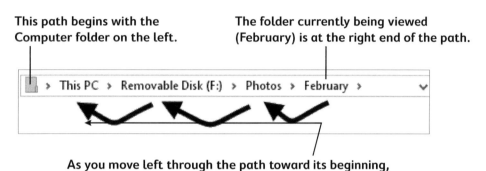

This path begins with the Computer folder on the left.

The folder currently being viewed (February) is at the right end of the path.

As you move left through the path toward its beginning, you are navigating up the folder structure.

Navigating via the Address Bar

The subfolders listed in the path actually are buttons that, when clicked, open that subfolder in the folder window. Each subfolder in the path also has a drop-down menu that shows its subfolders (accessed with the menu button). The subfolders on the drop-down menu also display in the folder window if clicked. You can navigate (browse) the folder structure of the path using these subfolder buttons and drop-down menus.

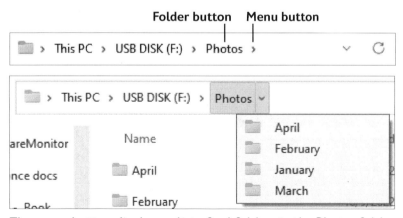

Folder button   Menu button

The menu button displays a list of subfolders in the Photos folder.

NAVIGATING WITH THE ADDRESS BAR PATH	
Task	**Procedure**
Move to a different folder on the path	▪ Move your mouse pointer over a folder name on the path to see its button and then click. Photos ▸
Move to a subfolder in a folder on the path	▪ Move your mouse pointer over the menu button ▸ and then click. ▪ Click a subfolder on the drop-down list. 📁 January

HANDS-ON 6.3 Navigate Using the Address Bar

In this exercise, you will use the address bar to navigate within your personal folders.

1. Click the **File Explorer** icon on the taskbar.

2. Follow these steps to navigate to the Pictures folder:

Ⓐ Click the menu button ▸ on the address bar to the right of the Home icon.

When you click the menu button it points down instead of to the right.

Ⓑ Choose the **This PC** folder from the list.

3. Click the menu button ▸ to the right of *This PC* on the address bar and choose **Pictures**.

The View pane displays the contents of the Pictures folder, and the folder's name is added to the path on the address bar.

4. Close File Explorer.

The Back and Forward Buttons

The Back and Forward buttons remember the order of the folders that you have viewed. If you choose to view a subfolder and then change your mind, the Back button will change your view back to your previous folder.

If you change your mind again, you can return to the subfolder you were just viewing by using the Forward button. The buttons work a lot like the back and forward buttons on a DVD player's remote control that allow you to move back and forth through the frames of a movie.

- The Back button takes you back to previously viewed locations in the reverse order of the way they were originally viewed.
- The Forward button doesn't work until you move back at least one step. (This is why that button is usually grayed out.)

Tip! The Back and Forward buttons in Microsoft Edge work just like the buttons in a folder window.

HANDS-ON 6.4 Use the Back and Forward Buttons

In this exercise, you will use the Back and Forward buttons in a folder window to navigate folders.

1. Click the **File Explorer** icon on the taskbar.

2. Double-click the **Pictures** folder.
   The View pane (right panel) now displays the contents of the Pictures folder. Notice that the Forward button is faded, which indicates the button is inactive. The Forward button won't work until you use the Back button at least once.

3. Click the **Back** button to move back into Pictures.
   Windows returns you to the previous view—in this case, Pictures. Notice that the Forward button is now colored, indicating that it is active.

4. Click the **Forward** button to return to the Pictures folder.
   Windows moves you forward to the folder from which you had moved back, which in this case is to the Pictures folder.

5. Close **File Explorer**.

Units of Measure for Computer Storage

Size and capacity in the computer world are based on the byte, which is the smallest unit of measurement in the computer world. When you are typing a letter, each character you type is one byte of information.

Measurement	Abbreviations	Is Equal to...
Byte		1 character (e.g., a, b, !, etc.)
Kilobyte	KB or "K"	1,024 bytes
Megabyte	MB or "meg"	1,024 kilobytes
Gigabyte	GB or "gig"	1,024 megabytes
Terabyte	TB	1,024 gigabytes

Note! This note is especially for math junkies! Notice that all the numbers end in 24. This is because computer numbers tend to be based on factors of 8. To simplify these numbers, they are often rounded to the nearest thousand.

Common Data File Sizes

Different types of data that you create will require different amounts of storage space. A basic rule of thumb is that the more complicated the file, the more space it needs. A photo will need more space than a typed document; a home video will need more space than a photo.

Item	Approximate Size
Word-processing document	20–30 K per page
Digital camera photo	1–7 MB, depending on your camera, the picture's quality, and its size
Music file	3–6 MB per song, depending on the audio quality and song length
Video file	1–20 MB for every 30 seconds, depending on the video's quality and format
HD video	1.7 MB per second or 50–55 MB per 30 seconds

The View Tab

The way folder and file information is displayed in File Explorer can be changed using commands in the View tab. Other commands in the View tab change how the information shown in the View pane is sorted.

The View commands change how files and folders are presented in the Folders pane. The various commands not only change the size of the file icons but also the amount of information shown for each file, folder, or drive.

As you work with files and folders, you may find that some views work better than others for various tasks.

Tip! Folder and drive windows remember their view settings when closed. You may want to change the view as you complete the exercises to more closely match the exercise figures.

Sorting

By default, most folders are sorted with subfolders showing first, followed by files. Everything is sorted alphabetically by name from A to Z. This arrangement can be changed using the Sort button.

With the Sort drop-down menu, you can choose from other key pieces of information to sort by and change from ascending to descending sort order. This can be very useful when looking for a specific file. For example, when you can't find a file you were just working on, you can sort by Date Modified, and files will be sorted with the ones most recently changed at the top of the window.

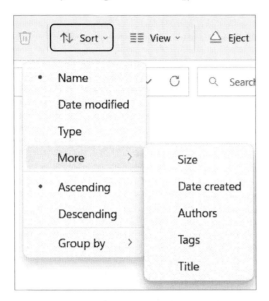

COMMON SORT FILTERS	
Filter	**Explanation**
Name	The default sort order for files in all folders
Date Modified	Sorts files by the last time they were changed (saved)
Type	Sorts files by type (e.g., all Paint files followed by all text files)
Size	Sorts files by their size
Ascending	Modifies the chosen sort; A–Z, smallest to biggest, etc. (Ascending is the default setting)
Descending	Modifies the chosen sort; Z–A, biggest to smallest, etc.

Tip! In some locations in File Explorer, when you work with drives or network locations, the list of filters on the Sort button may be different.

HANDS-ON 6.5 Sort Folders

In this exercise, you will sort the folders on the local disk (C: drive).

1. Click the **File Explorer** icon on the taskbar.

2. Click **This PC**.

3. Under the Devices and Drives section, double-click **Local Disk (C:)**. Your drive C: may have a different name.

File Explorer shows all the folders that contain Windows as well as the apps on your computer. By default they are in alphabetical order (unless someone else has changed the sort already).

4. Click **Sort** and choose **Date**.

   Notice the folders are now ordered by the date they were last changed.

5. Click **Sort→Name**.

6. Change the sort order from Ascending to **Descending**.

   Notice that the folders are now organized from Z–A.

7. Close File Explorer.

· ·

Identifying the Contents of a Folder

The icons used to identify folders can tell you a lot about the kind of information stored in that folder. Windows changes the look of a folder icon (in certain views) to help you identify whether it holds subfolders or files, as well as to indicate the file types. The folders will look different on each computer and may change over time, depending on the files available in the folder for making the representation and future updates to Windows.

The basic folder icon looks like a traditional tabbed manilla folder. A folder icon like this can mean the folder is empty. As of this writing, Windows also uses the basic folder icon for folders containing video files.

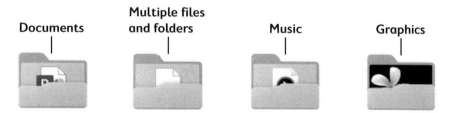

The folder icon can take on different looks to give you an idea of what files are within it.

The Folders Pane

The Folders pane enables you to select files from a more complete view of the folder "tree" (hierarchy), starting with This PC. The Folders pane displays all the drives and folders on your computer, plus any attached external drives and their folders. When you click a folder, the contents of that folder are displayed in the View pane to the right of the Folders pane.

The Folders pane is showing the hierarchy structure of all the drives and folders.

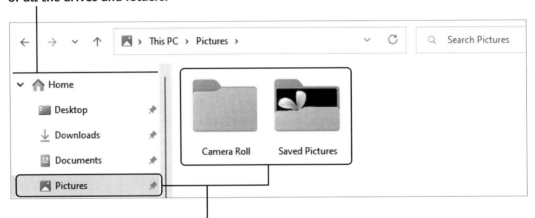

The contents of the selected drive or folder in the Folders pane are shown in the View pane to the right.

Expanding Subfolders

Some folders may have an expand view > button on the left. The expand view button enables you to see the subfolders in that folder. When clicked, the folder expands to show its subfolders without changing the View pane. When the arrow button is pointing down, it indicates that the folder is expanded.

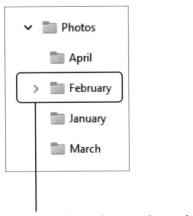

The expand view button shows that the folder has subfolders to view.

When the button is pointing down, the folder is expanded and you can see all the subfolders.

🖱 HANDS-ON 6.6 Navigate Using the Folders Pane

In this exercise, you will use the Folders pane to navigate among folders.

1. Click the **File Explorer** icon on the taskbar.

2. **Maximize** the folder window.

3. Follow these steps to navigate using the Folders pane:

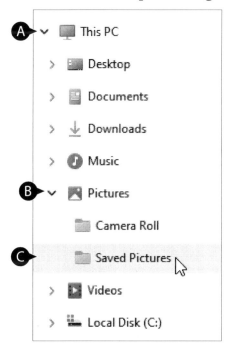

Ⓐ Click the expand view button next to *This PC* (if necessary) to expand the folder.

Ⓑ Click to expand **Pictures**.

Ⓒ Choose the **Saved Pictures** folder from the list.

The View pane now shows the contents of the Saved Pictures folder. Depending on what others have done on the computer, there may or may not be many (or even any) items in this folder.

4. Close the folder window.

Multiple Tabs in File Explorer

One of the newest features in File Explorer is tabs. Tabs enable you to have multiple Explorer views open without having to open multiple copies of File Explorer. You can use tabs to look at multiple file locations at once, to copy and move files around, and to open multiple files from various locations.

You add a tab using the plus sign icon to the right of the open tab(s). You can close individual tabs using the familiar X icon.

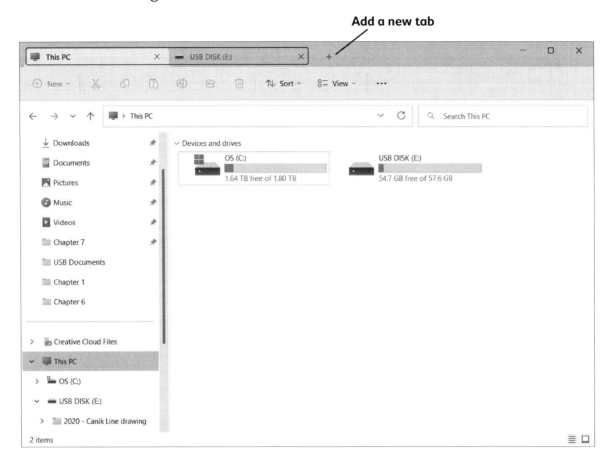

Add a new tab

HANDS-ON 6.7 Open Multiple Tabs in File Explorer

In this exercise you will open multiple tabs in File Explorer.

1. Open File Explorer and click **This PC**.

2. On the tabs bar click the plus (+) icon to add a new tab.

3. Click the new tab to select it and then click back on the **This PC** tab.
   Notice how easily you can move back and forth between the tabs.

4. Close File Explorer.

Searching for Files

Windows' Search feature allows you to easily look for lost files or folders. By typing in part of a filename or some text from a file, Search displays (filters) the files and folders it finds that match your search text. Search can help you locate any type of file including music, graphics, and text files.

By default, Search automatically looks at files in the folder you are currently viewing, plus all of your personal folders, including Documents, Pictures, Music, and many more.

Windows gathers information about your various documents in the background while you work. This information is collected in a large index that makes Search work faster and more accurately.

When you start typing search words into the Search box, Windows displays all related files and folders.

The green bar shows the progress of your search.

Note! Search may not seem important now, but as your music library grows or you start using a digital camera, the number of files in your personal folders may blossom into the thousands. Without Search, finding lost files could become tedious.

⌕ HANDS-ON 6.8 Find a File with Windows Search

In this exercise, you will use Search to locate all text files on This PC.

1. Click the **File Explorer** icon on the taskbar.

2. Click **This PC**.

3. Type **txt** in the Search box.

Notice that as you start typing text, Windows immediately starts looking for files and folders that match your search.

4. Click the **Close** button at the end of the Search box to return to displaying all files in This PC.

5. Close File Explorer.

· ·

Self-Assessment

To check your knowledge of the key concepts introduced in this chapter, complete this Self-Assessment quiz.

1. You can securely remove a USB flash drive by unplugging it at any time.   **true   false**

2. You can use Search to find music and pictures as well as documents.   **true   false**

3. Every login name has its own personal folders.   **true   false**

4. USB flash drives are often called thumb drives.   **true   false**

5. Folders can contain other folders (subfolders).   **true   false**

6. By default, Search will look for files only in the folder you are currently viewing.   **true   false**

7. You can navigate to drives and folders using all of the following except the _____.

   A. address bar

   B. Folders pane

   C. Search pane

   D. Back and Forward buttons

8. In a folder window, you can navigate to various folders using the _____.

   A. address bar

   B. Back and Forward buttons

   C. Folders pane

   D. All of the above

9. How big is the average music file?

   A. 3–6 MB

   B. 1–20 MB

   C. 30 K

   D. 1.7 MB

10. A USB flash drive is a(n) _____.

    A. removable storage device

    B. internal storage device

    C. temporary storage device

    D. network storage device

⚙ Skill Builders

SKILL BUILDER 6.1 Find the Remaining Capacity of a Drive

In this exercise, you will explore your USB flash drive. First you'll discover which folders and files are stored on the drive.

1. Click the **File Explorer** icon on the taskbar.

2. Plug your USB flash drive into a USB port on the computer.

   Depending on how it is configured, Windows probably will open an AutoPlay window asking what you want to do with the newly plugged-in drive.

3. Click **This PC** and then navigate to your USB drive.

4. Double-click on the icon for your **USB flash drive**.

   Are there any subfolders? What file types (data, photos, music) have you copied to the drive?

5. Open any folders on your USB flash drive to see what data has been stored, or continue with the next step if there aren't any folders on the drive.

Find Out How Much Free Space Is Available

Now you will give a command to display the available space on your USB flash drive.

6. Click **This PC**.

7. Right-click the **USB flash drive** icon and choose **Properties**.

Windows displays a pie chart and details about the storage space on your flash drive.

The Properties dialog box shows how much space is used and how much is available.

8. Click **OK**.

9. Close File Explorer.

SKILL BUILDER 6.2 Search the Contents of Files

In this exercise, you will find files by looking for content within the file itself.

1. Click the **File Explorer** icon on the taskbar.

2. Click **This PC**.

3. If necessary, click the **See More** (three ellipses) button.

4. Choose **Options→Search** and, if necessary, click to add a check mark next to the option to always search the names and contents of files. Click **OK** to exit.

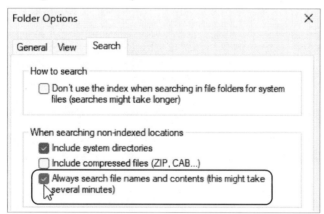

The file search will now look for search terms within document-type files.

5. Click in the **Search** box and type: `internet`

Depending on the number of files on your computer, the search may take some time. Notice that the files being shown don't necessarily have the word internet *in their filename.*

6. Click the **Close** button on the Search box.

7. Choose **Options→Search** and make sure the option to always search is not checked. (If it is, remove it.) Click **OK** to exit.

We don't want to leave this option on, as it will slow down future searches.

8. Close File Explorer.

CHAPTER 7

Storing Files

LEARNING OBJECTIVES

- Create new folders and subfolders for organizing your files

- Move or copy folders and files from one location to another

- Delete folders and files and, if necessary, restore them from the Recycle Bin

- Use OneDrive to store your files and folders

- Upload to and download from OneDrive

At some point after you have saved drawings from Paint and letters from Word or transferred pictures from your digital camera, you will want to organize these digital files. Windows provides methods for organizing files that are similar to how you would organize a filing cabinet in an office. In this chapter, you will create folders, move files around between folders, and work with the Recycle Bin to retrieve accidently deleted files. You will also spend time organizing files on OneDrive, your cloud storage location.

Learning Resources: **boostyourskills.lablearning.com**

📂 Case Study: Getting Organized

Aileen has been creating and saving many different file types on her computer. She has lots of pictures from her digital camera, a large collection of her favorite songs, all kinds of homework from a half dozen classes—and a big mess. Her photos are stuffed into the Pictures folder like pictures thrown in a shoebox. Her music collection is reasonably organized, but she would like to put some of the songs online so she can listen to them at work. The biggest mess is her homework. It has all been saved in her Documents folder, but assignments from different classes are all mixed together. She wants all the homework from each class to be grouped, so she can easily find an assignment when she needs it.

Aileen has learned how to make subfolders. She decides to organize her personal folders the same way she would organize a filing cabinet. In Documents, she creates a subfolder for each semester, makes a subfolder for each class within the semester folders, and then moves the appropriate files into each folder. For her pictures, she creates folders for different years and months in the Pictures folder. She also creates copies of pictures she used for homework and puts the copies into the class subfolders.

Aileen is pleased with her first attempt at organizing her files.

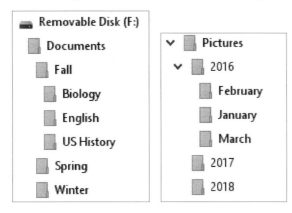

Creating Folders

The purpose of having folders in the Windows system is to make it easier to organize the thousands of files on your computer. Electronic folders enable you to organize files into groups, such as a folder for your Maui pictures or one for your science projects. Although each person will have their own organizational style, certain conventions must be followed as you create new folders:

- Folders can be created in another folder, on a drive, on OneDrive, or on the Desktop.
- The naming conventions for folders are the same as those for naming files. Refer to the "Naming Files" table in Chapter 4. A folder name (including its entire path) can be up to 255 characters long and include some symbols, such as dashes, commas, ampersands, and apostrophes.
- You cannot have two folders with identical names in the same location. Windows will merge the two folders.

Creating New Folders

There are two commonly used procedures for creating new folders: using the New Folder button in the folder window and choosing from the pop-up menu (also called a right-click menu).

CREATING FOLDERS	
Task	**Procedure**
Create a new folder via the New Folder button	<ul><li>Open the folder or drive where you want to put a new folder.</li><li>Choose Home→New→New Folder from the Ribbon.</li><li>Type the new folder name and tap Enter.</li></ul>
Create a new folder via the right-click method	<ul><li>Navigate to the location (Desktop, folder, or drive) where you want to put a new folder.</li><li>Right-click a blank place in the window or on the Desktop and choose New→Folder.</li><li>Type the new folder name and tap Enter.</li></ul>

Note! The Desktop is a folder that can be viewed in a folder window, which is where the New Folder command will be available. However, usually you see the Desktop as your opening screen without menus, so in this case, use the right-click method to create a new folder.

How Files Are Stored in Your Computer

There is an order to how your computer stores files on its various internal and external drives. The process for storing files is similar to procedures you might use to organize a filing cabinet—individual files might be grouped by subject, put inside folders, and labeled with an appropriate name. If there are many files within a folder, you might create subfolders to subdivide the primary folder into more specific groups. The drives on a computer are organized in a similar manner, using electronic folders, subfolders, and files.

Folders and Subfolders Created by Windows

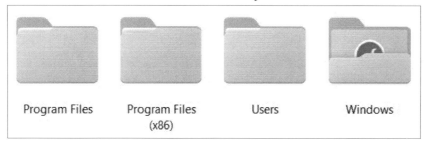

Program Files   Program Files   Users   Windows
(x86)

System folders installed on your local C: drive by Windows

Electronic folders, subfolders, and files are created when Windows is installed on the local hard drive (C:) of your computer. Windows is a very large collection of programs with thousands of system files that are stored on your internal hard drive. The purpose of the system files is to help the computer carry out all of the tasks necessary to run Windows.

Most of Windows' system files are stored in a folder named Windows. The files in the folder are grouped into several thousand subfolders. When a new application program is installed onto your hard drive, some of the program files may be stored in the Windows folder, but the rest of the files are grouped into a folder with a name chosen by the manufacturer. This folder is then stored in the folder named Program Files.

As new users are added to your computer, a subfolder for each—named after the user—is created inside Windows' Users folder. Windows also creates personal subfolders for each user to help them organize their documents, pictures, music, videos, and other common types of files.

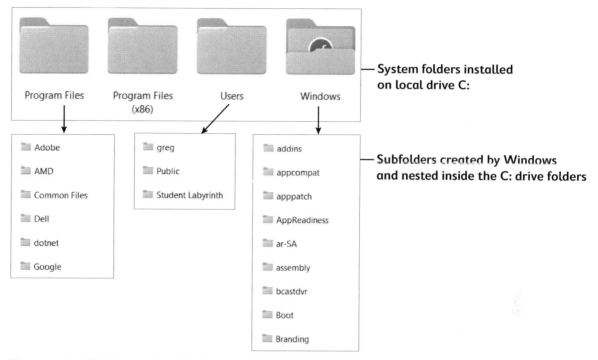

Thousands of folders and subfolders are created by Windows on your local hard drive.

Renaming Files and Folders

Sometimes you will want to correct or change the name of a file or folder. You must follow Windows' naming conventions, mentioned previously, when you do so. You also can select and rename multiple files or folders simultaneously. When you rename a folder with the name of an existing folder in the same location, Windows will ask if you want to merge the two folders.

RENAMING FILES OR FOLDERS	
Task	**Procedure**
Rename files or folders from a toolbar menu	▪ Open the file/folder location and select the item(s) to be renamed. ▪ Choose Home→Organize→Rename. ▪ Type the new name and tap Enter.
Rename files or folders using a right-click	▪ Open the file/folder location and select the item(s) to be renamed. ▪ Right-click a selected item and choose Rename. ▪ Type the new name and tap Enter.

🖰 HANDS-ON 7.1 Create a New Folder on the Desktop

In this exercise, you will create and name a new folder on the Desktop. Then you will rename it.

As there are no menus displayed on the Desktop for creating a folder, use the right-click method to display a pop-up menu that will allow you to create one.

1. Follow these steps to create a new folder on the Desktop:

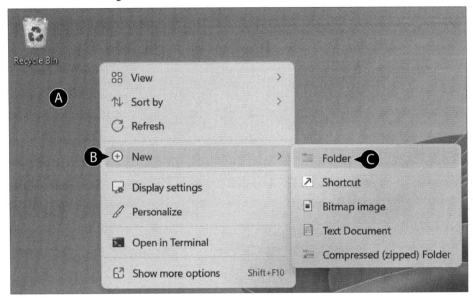

Ⓐ Right-click on a clear area of the Desktop to display its pop-up menu.

Ⓑ Choose **New**.

Ⓒ Click **Folder**.

The new folder appears with its name selected, ready for you to type a new one.

2. To name the folder, type **Practice** and tap ⎡Enter⎤.

3. Create another folder called **More Practice** and tap ⎡Enter⎤.

Rename the Folder

4. Right-click the **Practice** folder and choose **Rename**.

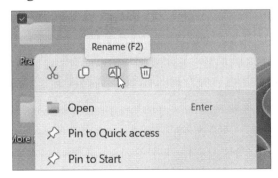

5. Type the new name **Delete Practice** and tap Enter.

6. Right-click the **More Practice** folder and rename it: **Junk Folder**

Creating Subfolders

When a folder gets filled with files, you may wish to divide the files into groups using subfolders. Those subfolders can have their own subfolders, and so on. Subfolders are also called *nested* folders. When a new login name, such as Student, is created, Windows creates a User folder named Student along with a bunch of subfolders (including Documents, Pictures, and Music) that are nested inside. If you then nest two subfolders named Animals and Flowers inside the Pictures folder, the *path* (hierarchy) looks like this:

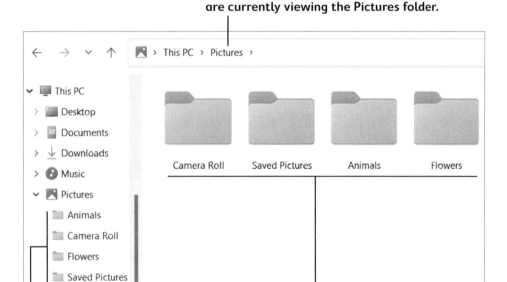

The address bar path shows that you are currently viewing the Pictures folder.

The Pictures folder has folders nested inside, as displayed in the View pane.

The View pane also displays the nested folders.

 HANDS-ON 7.2 Create Folders on Your Flash Drive

In this exercise, you will create two new folders on your USB flash drive.

1. Connect your USB flash drive to a USB port.

   Wait a moment for the computer to recognize the USB flash drive. Depending on your USB flash drive, a "tap to choose…" message may appear in the bottom-right corner of the screen. Ignore it, and it will disappear after a few moments.

   > **Removable Disk (F:)**
   > Tap to choose what happens with removable drives.

2. Click the **File Explorer** icon on the taskbar.

3. Click your **USB flash drive**.

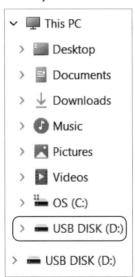

   Windows displays the contents of your USB flash drive. Notice the drive name and letter in the address bar path. (Your name and drive letter will probably differ from what's shown here.)

Create a New Folder

Now that you have navigated to your USB flash drive, you are ready to create folders on it. The New Folder command always creates the new folder at your current location.

4. Follow these steps to create and name a new folder:

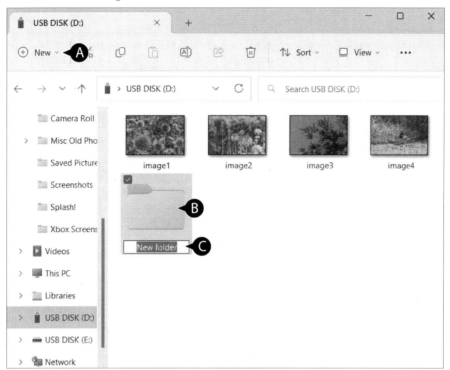

Ⓐ Choose **New**→**Folder**.

Ⓑ Notice the new folder in the View pane. The folder name is highlighted, ready for you to give it a new name.

Ⓒ Type **Photos** to replace the temporary name *New Folder* and tap Enter.

5. Double-click the new **Photos** folder to open it.

The folder is empty, so nothing displays in the View pane.

6. Click the **Back** ← button.

The View pane displays the contents of your USB flash drive. The Photos folder has moved to the top of the list, and this is because Windows normally displays folders before any files.

Create an Additional Folder

7. Choose **New**→**Folder**.

8. Name the new folder **USB Documents** and tap Enter.

Moving and Copying Folders and Files

From time to time you may want to reorganize your folders and files. You can easily move folders and files to a new location or put copies of folders or files in other locations.

The Cut, Copy, and Paste Method

To cut and paste or copy and paste folders and files, you use methods similar to those used for text and objects in Chapter 4, "Working with Apps." Take time to compare the similarities and differences. As with text, you must select at least one folder or file before you can give the Cut or Copy command. You will learn how to select more than one folder or file at a time later in this chapter.

The Cut, Copy, and Paste commands are conveniently located on the menu bar at the top of the window.

How the Commands Work

The following applies to folders and files being cut or copied and then pasted within a folder window:

- **Cut:** Deletes the selected file/folder from its present location only *after* a copy of that file/folder is pasted into a new location.
- **Copy:** Leaves the selected file/folder in its present location when a copy is pasted into a new location.
- **Paste:** Inserts a copy of the last file/folder that was cut or copied into the folder/drive currently open.
- **Undo:** Reverses your most recent Paste command.

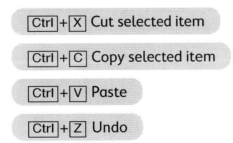

[Ctrl]+[X] Cut selected item

[Ctrl]+[C] Copy selected item

[Ctrl]+[V] Paste

[Ctrl]+[Z] Undo

More About the Paste Command

A few additional features of the Paste command are useful to know:

- You can paste only once if you cut a file or folder.
- You can paste more than once if you copy a file or folder.
- You can usually use the Undo command if you paste a file or folder into an incorrect location.

USING CUT, COPY, AND PASTE WITH FILES/FOLDERS	
Task	Procedure
Move folders/files with Cut and Paste	<ul><li>Select the folder/file to move and choose Home→Clipboard→Cut.</li><li>Move to the new location (the Desktop, a folder, or a drive) and choose Home→Clipboard→Paste.</li></ul>
Copy folders/files with Copy and Paste	<ul><li>Select the folder/file to copy and choose Home→Clipboard→Copy.</li><li>Move to the new location (the Desktop, a folder, or a drive) and choose Home→Clipboard→Paste.</li></ul>
Undo a Paste command	<ul><li>After pasting in error, immediately choose Undo from the Quick Access toolbar.</li></ul>

HANDS-ON 7.3 Organize Folders Using Cut, Copy, and Paste

In this exercise, you will copy a file, paste the copy into a different location, and move a file using Cut and Paste.

Before You Begin: You will be using folders created earlier in this chapter as well as files you saved in Chapter 4, "Working with Apps." Your flash drive should still be connected.

1. Start File Explorer, if necessary, and click your **USB flash drive**.

2. Follow these steps to copy a file into a folder:

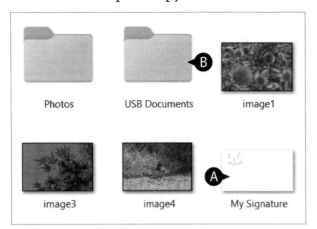

Photos   USB Documents   image1

image3   image4   My Signature

Ⓐ Click the **My Signature** file to select it and then choose **Copy**.

Ⓑ Double-click the **USB Documents** folder to open it and then choose **Paste**.

3. Click the **Back** ← button on the toolbar.

   Windows moves you out of the folder, back to viewing your USB flash drive. The original My Signature file is still on the drive.

4. Double-click the **USB Documents** folder to reopen it.

5. Select the **My Signature** file.

6. Choose **Delete**.

7. From the Delete File prompt that appears, choose **Yes**.

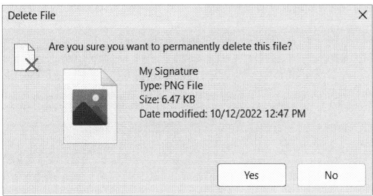

8. Click the **Back** button to view your USB flash drive window.

   The original My Signature file is still on the drive.

Cut and Paste Method

9. Click the **My Signature** file and then choose **Cut**.

10. Double-click the **USB Documents** folder to open it.

11. Choose **Paste**.

12. Click the **Back** button on the toolbar to return to the drive window.

    The My Signature file is no longer on the drive; it has been moved.

. . . .

The Drag-and-Drop Method

You used drag and drop in Chapter 5, "Using Email," to move emails to folders. Folders and files in the same locations can easily be moved or copied using drag and drop.

When you drag and drop a folder or file onto another folder or different drive, Windows does something very helpful. If you hesitate over the new location, a ScreenTip displays the default action (Move or Copy) and the name of the folder or drive where the object is being dropped.

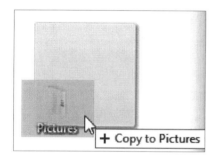

Although the left mouse button can be used to drag, it's better for new users to use the right mouse button when dragging and dropping folders/files because the right mouse button gives you more control over what will happen when you drop the folder or file. Using the right mouse button displays a menu when you release the button that allows you to choose a command to complete the procedure.

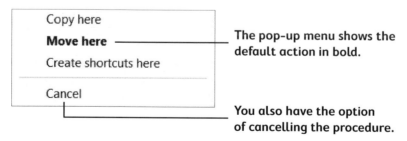

Using the right mouse button to drag and drop something to a new location lets you choose Copy Here or Move Here from a pop-up menu.

Tip! Develop good habits. Use the right mouse button to drag and drop because it gives you more control over the procedure and makes you less likely to make mistakes.

🖱 HANDS-ON 7.4 Copy and Move Files Using Drag and Drop

In this exercise, you will use your right mouse button with drag and drop to copy and move a file to another location on your USB flash drive.

1. Follow these steps to move and copy files using both drag and drop and the right mouse button:

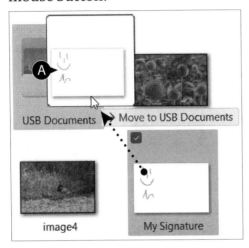
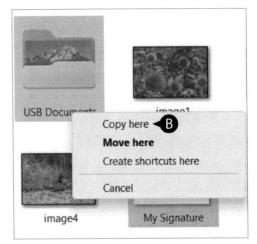

Ⓐ Place your mouse pointer over *My Signature*, hold down the right (not left) mouse button and drag over the **USB Documents** folder, and then release the mouse button.

Ⓑ Choose **Copy Here** from the pop-up menu.
The My Signature file is still on the drive window.

2. Double-click to open the **USB Documents** folder.
Notice that a copy of the My Signature file is now in the folder.

3. Select the **My Signature** file and choose **Delete**.

4. From the Delete File prompt that appears, choose **Yes**.

5. Click the **Back** ← button.

Move a File Using Drag and Drop

6. Using the right mouse button, drag the **My Signature** file onto the **USB Documents** folder and release the mouse button.
A pop-up menu appears, asking what you want to do with the file.

7. Choose **Move Here** from the pop-up menu.
The My Signature file disappears from view because it has been moved into a folder.

8. Double-click the **USB Documents** folder to open it.

The My Signature file is there, as you would expect.

9. Click the **Back** $\leftarrow$ button.

Selecting Multiple Files

You can select more than one folder or file at a time. When you select multiple folders or files, Windows lets you move or copy the whole group at the same time, which can save you a lot of time. It can also prevent you from making errors or forgetting files, which can happen if you move files one at a time.

SELECTING MULTIPLE FOLDERS AND FILES	
Task	**Procedure**
Select multiple contiguous folders/files	▪ Click the first folder/file. ▪ Hold down Shift, click the last folder/file in the group, and then release Shift. Note: Add additional folders/files to the selection by holding down Ctrl and clicking the desired items.
Select multiple noncontiguous folders/files	▪ Hold down Ctrl and then click each folder/file you wish to select once. Note: Click a selected item while holding down Ctrl to deselect it.
Select a group of folders/files by dragging	▪ Taking care not to point at any file/folder, place the tip of the mouse pointer below the last file/folder in the group of files/folders you wish to select. ▪ Drag with the left mouse button up and to the left to make a selection box large enough to select the group.
Selecting all folders/files	▪ Choose Home→Select→Select All, or hold down Ctrl and tap A.

🖱 HANDS-ON 7.5 Select and Move Multiple Items

In this exercise, you will move multiple items simultaneously using different methods. To begin, you will use the $\boxed{\text{Ctrl}}$ and $\boxed{\text{Shift}}$ keys.

1. Follow these steps to select multiple items using the $\boxed{\text{Shift}}$ key:

Ⓐ Click once (don't double-click) to select the **Photos** folder.

Ⓑ Hold down $\boxed{\text{Shift}}$, click once on **image2**, and then release $\boxed{\text{Shift}}$.

Notice that using the $\boxed{\text{Shift}}$ key selected the contiguous folders and files between the first and last selected items.

2. Follow these steps to select multiple items using the $\boxed{\text{Ctrl}}$ key:

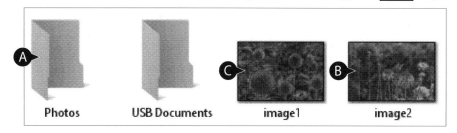

Ⓐ Click once on the **Photos** folder to deselect all items except Photos.

Ⓑ Hold down $\boxed{\text{Ctrl}}$ and click **image2** once to select it as well.

Ⓒ While holding down $\boxed{\text{Ctrl}}$, click **image1** once to add the file to the selection.

Notice that using $\boxed{\text{Ctrl}}$ lets you select noncontiguous items.

You also can combine the $\boxed{\text{Shift}}$ and $\boxed{\text{Ctrl}}$ key methods to select several files with $\boxed{\text{Shift}}$ and then select or deselect other folders and files with $\boxed{\text{Ctrl}}$.

Ⓓ Click somewhere in the window besides the items to deselect them.

Select Multiple Items by Dragging

3. Follow these steps to select multiple items:

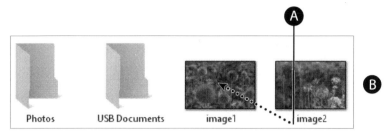

A Place the mouse pointer under image2, hold down the left mouse button, and drag a selection box that touches the **image2** and **image1** icons.

B Release the mouse button and notice that both files remain selected.

Move Multiple Files by Dragging

4. With the image1 and image2 files still selected, follow these steps to move the multiple selected files:

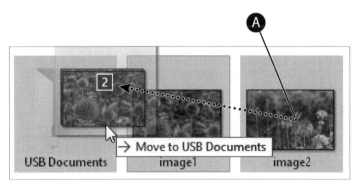 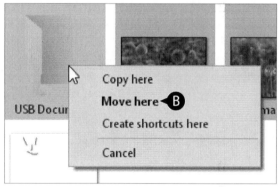

A Hold your mouse pointer over one of the selected icons, hold down the right mouse button, and drag the files over the **USB Documents** folder (notice the ScreenTip that appears).

B Release the mouse button and choose **Move Here**.

The files disappear from view as they are moved into the folder.

5. Double-click the **USB Documents** folder to open it and confirm that the files have been moved.

6. Close File Explorer.

Deleting and Restoring Folders and Files

Windows enables you to clean up your computer folders by deleting unwanted folders and files. Folders and files that are deleted from an internal or external hard drive are moved to the Recycle Bin folder. Folders and files in the Recycle Bin can later be returned to their original locations, if desired.

The Recycle Bin

The Recycle Bin is a unique folder and is important enough that Windows includes an icon linked to it on the Desktop. The Recycle Bin folder serves as a temporary storage place for folders and files deleted from hard disk drives.

It is like your recycle bin at home. When you put something into a recycle bin, it stays there unless you change your mind and retrieve it, or until it is permanently removed by the recycling truck. Likewise, folders and files sent to the Recycle Bin folder can be retrieved and sent back to their original locations (restored), but a folder or file that is deleted from the Recycle Bin is permanently deleted.

 If you right-click the Recycle Bin icon on the Desktop and choose Empty Recycle Bin, all of its folders and files will be permanently deleted.

Deleting Folders and Files

Only folders/files deleted from drives categorized by Windows as internal or external hard disk drives are moved to the Recycle Bin. However, folders/files deleted from drives categorized by Windows as devices with removable storage (such as USB flash drives and CD/DVD drives) *are not* moved to the Recycle Bin. These deleted folders and files are permanently deleted and cannot be restored.

Windows will display a Delete Folder dialog box similar to the following if the objects being deleted will not be sent to the Recycle Bin.

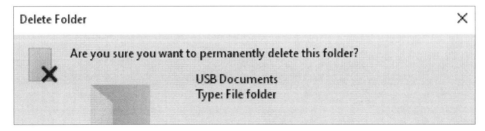

Delete Folder   ✕

Are you sure you want to permanently delete this folder?

✕   USB Documents
Type: File folder

 Note! USB flash drives normally show up as removable drives. Occasionally some will show up as hard drives. As a precaution, you should always assume that folders/files deleted from USB drives will be permanently deleted.

Restoring Folders and Files

Deleted folders/files moved to the Recycle Bin folder can be restored (moved back) to the original locations from which they were deleted. When the Recycle Bin is opened, there is a Restore All Items button on the Ribbon. The Restore button is used to initiate the restore, but its label will change depending on the number of items selected.

No items selected ——— 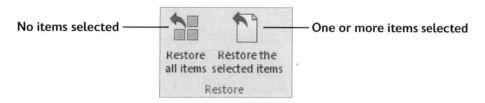 ——— One or more items selected

DELETING AND RESTORING FOLDERS AND FILES	
Task	**Procedure**
Delete a file or folder	■ Select the folder(s)/file(s) to delete. ■ Tap Delete ; choose Yes to confirm the deletion.
Open the Recycle Bin	■ Double-click the Recycle Bin icon.
Restore items from the Recycle Bin	■ Open the Recycle Bin. ■ If desired, select the item(s) to be restored, using Ctrl or Shift if necessary. ■ Choose Recycle Bin Tools→Restore→Restore All Items *or* Restore the Selected Items.
Empty the Recycle Bin	■ Double-click the Recycle Bin icon. ■ Choose Recycle Bin Tools→Manage→Empty Recycle Bin.

Warning! All folders and files in the Recycle Bin are permanently deleted when you choose Empty Recycle Bin.

HANDS-ON 7.6 Delete and Restore Folders or Files

In this exercise, you will delete a folder on the Desktop and then restore it.

Before You Begin: If there is not a folder titled *Delete Practice* on your Desktop, complete Hands-On 7.1 before continuing.

1. Click the **Delete Practice** folder on the Desktop to select it.

2. Tap the Delete key to delete it.
Now you will restore the folder back to the Desktop.

3. Double-click the **Recycle Bin** icon on the Desktop.

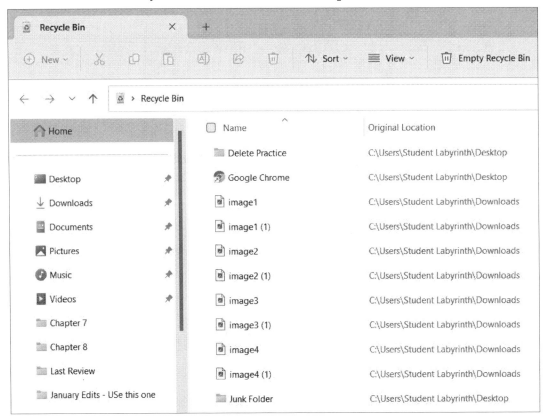

Windows opens a new folder window to display the contents of the Recycle Bin. Depending on what others have done on the computer, the folder may contain just the folder you deleted or many other folders and files as well.

4. Click the **Delete Practice** folder in the Recycle Bin. (You may need to scroll down the list to find it.)

5. Choose **Recycle Bin Tools→Restore→Restore the Selected Items**.

6. Close the Recycle Bin and confirm that the Delete Practice folder is restored to the Desktop.

OneDrive File Storage

OneDrive uses a simplified file system that is not much more complicated than the one used in Outlook. In fact, all of the concepts regarding files and folders that you have learned so far apply to OneDrive.

The biggest difference between OneDrive and your USB flash drive is that OneDrive is on the Internet and available from any of your computers and smartphones, whereas your USB flash drive is a physical item you carry with you.

Once you get used to using OneDrive, you may find that you no longer need to carry a USB flash drive.

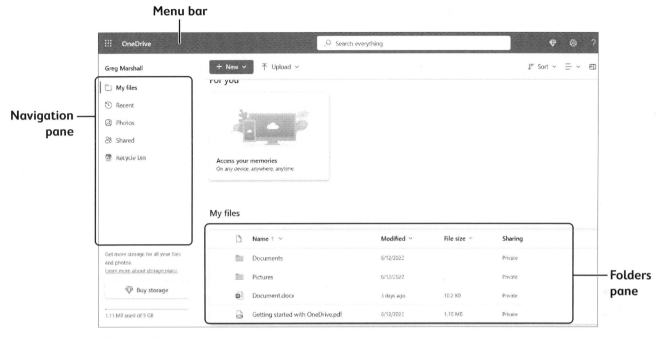

The OneDrive default screen as seen in your browser

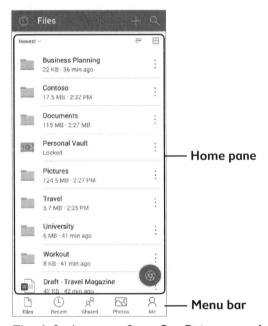

The default screen from OneDrive on an Android smartphone

Creating OneDrive Folders

OneDrive enables you to create folders for sorting stored files by using the New button. The drop-down menu on the New button also allows you to create blank new documents for other free Microsoft 365 online apps, including Word.

HANDS-ON 7.7 Create a OneDrive Folder

In this exercise, you will create a folder in OneDrive.

1. Start OneDrive.

2. Click the **New** button on the menu bar and then choose **Folder** from the drop-down menu.

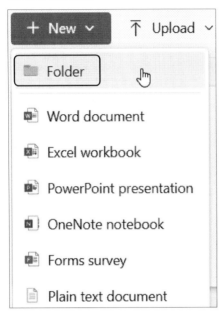

3. In the dialog box that appears, type **Uploaded Files** and click **Create**.

Notice that the folder appears in OneDrive.

4. Click the **Uploaded Files** folder once.
   The folder is empty.

5. Create another folder named: **Pictures**
   Pictures is now a subfolder of Uploaded Files.

6. Close OneDrive.

Navigating Between Folders

OneDrive, like File Explorer, uses a path to show where you are located in OneDrive. In OneDrive, clicking up the path is the easiest way to back out of a subfolder, as OneDrive has no button for going up one folder or a way to jump to the main view of OneDrive.

HANDS-ON 7.8 Move Between Folders

In this exercise, you will move around between folders on OneDrive.

1. Open OneDrive.

2. Click the **Uploaded Files** folder.

   Notice that the path shows you are in Uploaded Files.

3. Click the **Pictures** folder.

   My files > Uploaded Files > **Pictures**

   Notice that the path has grown to show you the Pictures folder.

4. On the path, click **Uploaded Files**.

   My files > Uploaded Files > **Pictures**

   The path now shows Uploaded Files as the end of the path and your current location.

5. Click **My Files**.

   You are now on the main screen of OneDrive.

6. Close OneDrive.

Tip! No matter how far down into the path of subfolders you are in, clicking My Files in OneDrive will always bring you back to the main screen.

Uploading Files to OneDrive

You can upload files from your computer to OneDrive with the click of a button. Files uploaded to OneDrive are immediately available to all of your computers and devices. Any file type can be uploaded, including documents, music files, images, and videos. When uploading, only a copy of the selected file is uploaded. The original is not moved.

Tip! You don't have to worry about file sizes because OneDrive recently raised the individual file size limit to 10 gigabytes per file, which is bigger than even a full-length movie file!

HANDS-ON 7.9 Upload to OneDrive

In this exercise, you will upload two files from your USB flash drive to OneDrive.

1. Start OneDrive and click the **Uploaded Files** folder. Make sure your USB flash drive is plugged in.

2. Click the **Upload** button on the menu bar and choose **Files**.
   An Open dialog box appears.

3. Follow these steps to choose a file to upload:

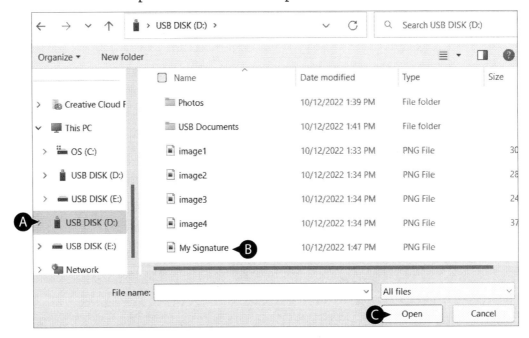

Ⓐ Choose your **USB flash drive** from the Navigation pane.

Ⓑ Choose the **My Signature** file in the Folders pane.

Ⓒ Click **Open**.

Watch as a message appears on the menu bar, showing that the upload is in progress. When it's complete, a pop-up message appears to let you know.

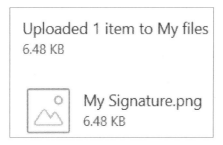

4. Follow steps 1–3 to upload the **image1** file to the **Uploaded Files** folder.
   Remember, image1 and image2 are now located in the USB Documents folder on your USB flash drive. Leave OneDrive open.

Downloading from OneDrive

Any files you have stored on OneDrive can be downloaded (copied) to your computer or device for use.

To download, you first need to select the file. OneDrive enables you to do this via a small round check box.

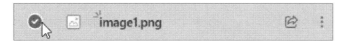

Selecting image1.png for download using the round check box

By default, files downloaded from OneDrive using the Microsoft Edge browser are put into the Downloads folder on your PC. Other browsers may download to a different location.

The ability to upload and download files enables you to have maximum flexibility when working with files. For example, you could create a file on a school computer, upload it to OneDrive, work on it from your smartphone on your bus ride home, and then download it to your laptop for final editing on your full version of Microsoft Word.

🖰 HANDS-ON 7.10 Download from OneDrive

In this exercise, you will download the Letter from Sylvia from OneDrive to your computer.

1. Click **My Files**.

2. Put your mouse pointer over the **Letter from Sylvia** and then click in the round check box that appears.

3. Click **Download** on the menu bar.

   The combination of OneDrive and the Microsoft Edge browser has placed a copy of your file in the Downloads folder on your computer.

4. Close any messages that appear along the bottom of the screen.

5. Close OneDrive and then open File Explorer.

6. Under Quick Access, double-click **Downloads**.

You should see the Letter from Sylvia.

7. Close File Explorer.

Self-Assessment

To check your knowledge of the key concepts introduced in this chapter, complete this Self-Assessment quiz.

1. The rules for naming folders are the same as those for naming files.   **true   false**

2. You can use the Cut and Paste commands to move folders/files from one location to another.   **true   false**

3. Deleted folders/files are always moved to the Recycle Bin.   **true   false**

4. If you delete a picture from the Desktop and then restore it, Windows restores it to the My Pictures folder. **true   false**

5. Folders and files deleted from a USB flash drive are not placed in the Recycle Bin.   **true   false**

6. Files stored on OneDrive can be accessed on any computer or device.   **true   false**

7. You can create new folders _____.

    A. in an existing folder

    B. on a drive

    C. on the Desktop

    D. All of the above

8. The Recycle Bin _____.

    A. includes an icon on the Desktop

    B. serves as a temporary holding area for deleted files and folders

    C. holds files and folders until they are permanently deleted or removed from the Recycle Bin

    D. All of the above

9. Multiple files and folders can be selected by _____.

    A. clicking them with Shift held

    B. clicking them with Ctrl held

    C. dragging across files/folders

    D. All of the above

10. One advantage of using OneDrive instead of a USB flash drive is _____.

    A. your OneDrive account has more storage space than your laptop

    B. OneDrive is available even with no Internet connection

    C. files are immediately available to all devices, including your smartphone

    D. None of the above

 # Skill Builders

SKILL BUILDER 7.1 Find and Copy Files

In this exercise, you will use the drag-and-drop method to move files into folders on OneDrive.

1. If necessary, open OneDrive.

2. Choose **New→Folder**.

3. Type **Letters** and then click **Create**.

4. Click and drag **Letter from Sylvia** onto the new **Letters** folder.

Notice that your mouse cursor shows your file being carried.

5. Click and drag **Office Manager Letter** to the **Letters** folder.

6. Click the **Letters** folder to view its contents.

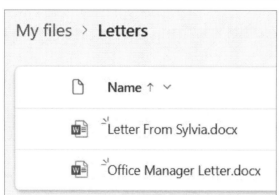

SKILL BUILDER 7.2 Open a File Directly from OneDrive

In this exercise, you will open a Word document directly from OneDrive and view it in Word.

1. Click the **Office Manager Letter**.

   Word automatically opens the document.

   Notice that you can also choose to open and edit the file in Word on your computer, if installed. Since Word was chosen, it is open, and your document is ready for editing.

2. Change *Sincerely* at the end of the letter to: **Thank you**

    Word saves your document as you work.

3. Close Word and OneDrive.

....

SKILL BUILDER 7.3 Create a File and Upload to OneDrive

When you are working on a project and intend to store files on OneDrive for easy access from anywhere, you may find that creating basic documents ahead of time helps you get organized. For example, you might create one file to hold the project description, another file to hold random notes, and another file to list citations and websites used for your research. In this exercise, you will create a basic file on your Desktop and upload it to OneDrive.

1. Right-click the **Desktop** and choose **New→Text Document**.

    A blank document appears on your Desktop.

2. Type **Research Notes** and press Enter.

    Notice that the default name of the file is replaced by your text.

3. Double-click the **Research Notes** file to open it.

4. Type: **Research Notes**

5. Choose **File→Save**.

6. Close the file.

7. Start OneDrive.

8. Click the **Upload** button and choose **Files**.

9. Follow these steps to upload the Research Notes file:

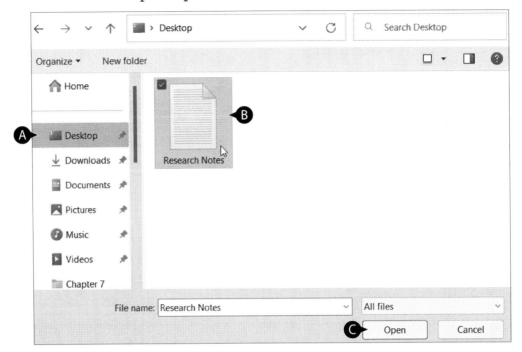

Ⓐ Choose **Desktop** from the Navigation pane.

Ⓑ Click **Research Notes**.

Ⓒ Click **Open**.

10. Close OneDrive after the upload is complete.

UNIT 3: THE INTERNET AND MORE

In the first two chapters in this unit, you will learn how to connect to, use, perform searches in, and protect yourself from threats when using the Internet and, in particular, Microsoft's Edge browser. You will find that the Internet allows you to access information, pictures, movies, music, games, and much more. In Chapter 10, you will learn more about adjusting the settings on your computer, how to keep your apps up to date, and how to use Microsoft's Store.

CHAPTER 8

Using the Internet

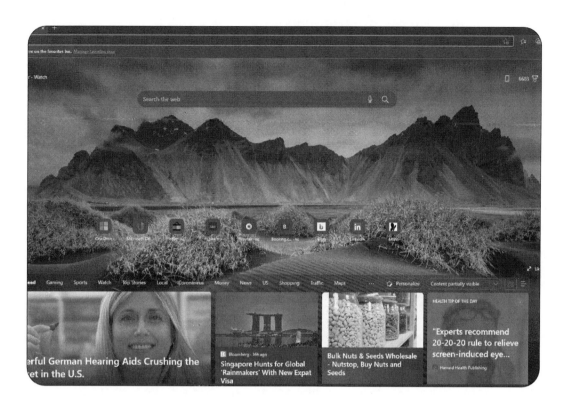

LEARNING OBJECTIVES

- Use a World Wide Web address to go directly to a website
- Identify the main components of a web address
- Use Microsoft Edge to browse the web
- Create a favorite with Microsoft Edge

Connecting to the Internet has become one of the primary reasons for owning a computer and learning to use computer technology. The Internet provides you with access to a wealth of information on almost any topic; entertainment, pictures, movies, music, and games; and the ability to shop the world from your home. In this chapter, you will use Microsoft Edge to browse the web.

Learning Resources: **boostyourskills.lablearning.com**

📂 Case Study: Browsing on the Web

Patrick is planning a trip to Arizona and figures most of the information he needs is available on the Internet. He uses Microsoft Edge to browse the Internet and searches using the term *grand canyon*.

grand canyon	🎤 🔍

He finds an amazing amount of information. One of the first pages listed is the official National Park Service site for the Grand Canyon (www.nps.gov/grca).

Grand Canyon National Park (U.S. National Park Service)
https://www.nps.gov/grca/index.htm ▾

Grand Canyon National Park. **Grand Canyon National Park**, in northern Arizona, encompasses 278 miles (447 km) of the Colorado River and adjacent uplands. Located on the ancestral ...

Plan Your Visit
Grand Canyon National Park, in northern ...
Mule Trips · Backcountry Hiking · River Trip

Lodging
Grand Canyon Chamber & Visitor's Bureau
P.O. Box 3007 Grand Canyon, AZ 86023 ...

Fees & Passes

Info

The National Park Service web page has information on everything Patrick needs: hotels, restaurants, events, and things to do. There are links to make reservations, helpful information, maps, and beautiful pictures. This site is going to make planning his trip easier, so he adds the web page to his favorites.

The Internet

The Internet has been in existence for more than 50 years. In its infancy, it was text based and was used primarily by the military and educational institutions. Using the Internet often involved typing long strings of text on a black screen (see the following illustration). That changed in the early 1990s, with the creation of the World Wide Web. The World Wide Web simplifies access to information through an interface that includes colored graphics and point-and-click links. Users don't have to remember and type complex addresses or know specifically where information is located; they can just point and click on links or onscreen buttons to jump to the information. This makes the Internet easier to use, more colorful, and more interesting.

This is Victoria Free-Net accessed using an older, text-based technology (Telnet, top left) and with a newer graphical browser technology (Internet Explorer, bottom right).

The World Wide Web

By far the most dominant segment of the Internet is the World Wide Web (WWW), commonly referred to as the **web**. The web is only one of many technology pieces that make up the Internet, but it has become the most commonly used because of its simplicity and graphic features.

Today's web pages have colorful multimedia displays and easy-to-click links to other web pages. Most people can access the web by learning some simple skills and understanding a few basic concepts.

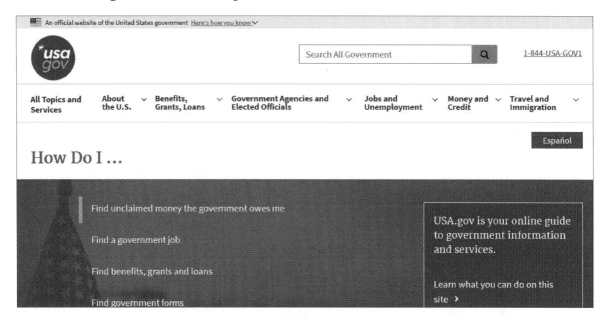

Equipment Used to Connect to the Internet

You need specific equipment to connect to the Internet. New computers typically include most of the equipment needed, but some equipment may be provided to you by your **Internet service provider (ISP)**.

Modems

A *modem* (stands for **mod**ulate/**dem**odulate) enables your computer to connect to the Internet via a standard telephone line. The original dial-up modems convert the analog signals of the phone system into the digital signal your computer uses. Once connected to a phone line, your computer can dial the phone number of your ISP to gain access to the Internet. Dial-up modem connections are slow compared to the high-speed connection options available in most parts of the country today, and they are used when other options are not available.

A high-speed modem converts the signals sent over telephone lines, over cable lines, or from a satellite into signals your computer can use to communicate with the Internet. It is called a high-speed modem because it moves data to and from your computer at a much faster rate than an earlier dial-up modem.

Routers

Once you have an Internet connection, a **router** enables you to connect multiple devices to that connection. A typical router will allow four devices to be networked together with network cables so they can all access the Internet.

A common Motorola cable modem and router

A wireless router works just like a regular router, with the added benefit of allowing access to the Internet via a wireless connection. Most laptop computers now have wireless capability; they can connect wirelessly at home or other locations that make their wireless routers available to the public, such as coffee shops, restaurants, and hotels. Many routers now combine the modem, router, and wireless router into one unit.

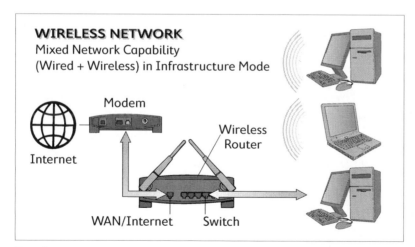

In infrastructure mode, a router or access point handles all network traffic.

Note! New technologies for connecting to the Internet emerge all the time. How Internet service is delivered keeps changing, most recently with the advent of high-speed phone-based connections including the newest standard of 5G. The way the service is used also changes and now it is being accessed from household appliances, automobiles, and smart devices like the Amazon Echo and Google Nest.

Connection Types

Connection to the Internet is made possible through a business known as an ISP (Internet service provider). Connecting to a service provider can be accomplished in several ways:

- via a telephone line using a dial-up modem
- via a telephone line using a high-speed modem (DSL)
- via a TV cable using a high-speed modem
- via a network at work or school
- via wireless connections, such as satellites, cell towers, and dish systems

Internet Service Providers

An ISP provides the connection between you and the Internet. The ISP is usually paid a monthly fee to maintain your connection. Many ISPs provide other services as well, and they might provide Internet services as part of a bundle of multiple services.

Most people now get their Internet connection from their cable or phone provider. That wasn't always the case. In the early days of the Internet, many ISPs were local businesses run by technology people. Some users are opting to return to local small businesses over large corporations, much in the same way they choose independent, local shops for their groceries, home goods, and other items. To find a local ISP, do a web search!

In most cases, the ISP will provide you with software that will automatically configure your computer with the correct settings for your new Internet connection as well as instructions for setting up any needed equipment.

Dial-Up Connections

A dial-up connection was the first type of Internet connection available to home consumers. It uses a dial-up modem and a standard phone line (sometimes referred to as POTS, for "plain old telephone system"). Dial-up gets its name from the fact that special software in your computer has to dial a phone number to make the connection.

High-Speed Connections

High-speed is a generic term for services that provide information transfer rates that are higher than typical dial-up transfer rates. You can access high-speed connections through your TV cable, phone line (referred to as digital subscriber line, or DSL), or even satellite dish.

High-speed connections can be more than 1000 times faster than dial-up connections. This means that a document that would take you 20 minutes to download over a dial-up connection might take only a couple seconds with a high-speed connection.

Network Connections

When you use a computer at work or school, you are connected to the Internet through a network. Connection to the Internet through a network allows you to move more data at a higher speed (more **bandwidth**) and to share that information with many computers at the same time. The Internet itself is a network of networks.

Wireless Connections

Wireless connections have become popular for an obvious reason—there is no wire. That means you do not have to be tied to a desk; you can be mobile and still be connected to the Internet.

Connection Speeds

Connections are measured in kilobits per second. High-speed connections may reference their speed in megabits. One megabit equals 1,000 kilobits.

Connection type	Speed	Example
Dial-up connection	56 kilobits	<ul><li>5–7 seconds to view an average web page</li><li>20–30 minutes to download one song</li></ul>
High-speed connection	20–300 megabits	<ul><li>1–2 seconds to view an average web page</li><li>15–20 seconds to download a song</li><li>Less than 30 minutes to download a movie</li></ul>

Web Browsers

Once you're connected to the web, you need a web **browser** to explore it. The web is like a very large coffee table book—it contains millions of pages filled with vibrant pictures, text, videos, and sounds on any topic you can think of. The browser lets you explore this "book," by jumping from page to page using special text and graphics that link you to other pages. There are many different browsers, and you can choose the one you want to use. You may also have more than one browser on your computer or device.

Microsoft Edge

The exercises in this book use Microsoft Edge, which is Microsoft's newest browser and replaces Internet Explorer as the default browser for Microsoft. Microsoft Edge comes installed on all versions of Windows. You have already used the Microsoft Edge browser in previous chapters for accessing OneDrive and Outlook.

Note! You will notice that the Microsoft Edge icon looks a lot like the Explorer icon. Microsoft did this on purpose to show the heritage of Microsoft Edge and to ease the transition for those individuals who have used Explorer for many years.

Internet Explorer

Internet Explorer was one of the dominant browsers for many years and has been the browser of choice for many schools and corporations. You will find Internet Explorer on most PCs, as it was the default browser for Windows up to version 8.1.

With Windows 11, Edge is now the default browser, and Internet Explorer is no longer supported.

Chrome

One of the dominant browsers available, Chrome was created by Google and is very popular among Google fans. Chrome is available at: google.com/chrome

Firefox

One of the most popular alternatives, Firefox is a free browser that you can download and use on your Windows computer. Firefox is available at: mozilla.com

Other Browsers

There are dozens of other browsers available on the Internet, including browsers that have specific functions or browsers that work on specific devices or smartphones. Other browsers you may hear mentioned include:

- Safari
- Chromium
- Android's browser

One of the great features of the Internet is the ability to explore and discover many new pieces of software and various ways to accomplish the digital tasks you need to complete.

Uniform Resource Locators (URLs)

In order for a browser to find specific websites, there needs to be a way to uniquely identify them. Every site on the Internet has a **Uniform Resource Locator (URL)**, which is also referred to as an address. You use the address to find and display a particular website (location). It's similar to finding a house by looking for its unique address, and just like houses, no two websites can have the same address.

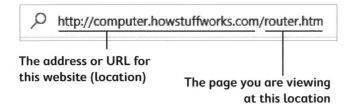

The address or URL for this website (location)

The page you are viewing at this location

Top-Level Domains

Website addresses are divided into major **domains**. The original six domains were used to divide Internet addresses into groups of websites with a common purpose. These domains are used mainly by American websites, because the US government was their creator and manager. As the web has gotten more popular, more and more foreign websites are using these major domains because of their global commercial success. The domain appears at the end of a web address.

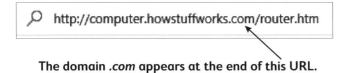

The domain *.com* appears at the end of this URL.

THE ORIGINAL TOP-LEVEL DOMAINS

Top-Level Domain	Designation	Notes
.com	Commercial	The most commonly used domain, open to any business, organization, or individual.
.edu	Education	Used by educational institutions, such as schools and colleges. There are special requirements for groups wanting to use this domain.
.gov	Government	Federal, state, and local government websites have this domain. It ensures that the information you are viewing is official government information, something that can be hard to tell with some .com websites.
.org	Organization	This domain was once reserved for nonprofit organizations, but today anybody can register for .org names.
.net	Internet	In times past, this domain was used mostly for Internet-related companies, but as businesses have increasingly had trouble finding good web addresses ending in .com, they have turned to .net.
.mil	Military	One of the least used domains on the Internet; reserved for the American military. Why does the military get their own top-level domain? The early research that created the Internet was funded by the Advance Research Projects Agency, ARPA.

These original top-level domains were the only ones used for over twenty years. In the last few years, though, a flood of new domain names has been created. Currently, there are more than one thousand top-level domains. A complete list of top-level domains, including recently added domains, can be found at: en.wikipedia.org/wiki/List_of_Internet_top-level_domains

Country Codes

Country codes also are top-level domains and consist of two-letter abbreviations that appear at the end of an address. Every country in the world has been assigned a country code that can be used in the creation of web addresses. Although addresses with country codes are not as common, you will find more of them as you research outside commercial and American websites.

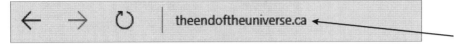

This web address ends in *.ca*, which is the country code for Canada.

SOME COMMON COUNTRY CODES			
Country	Code	Country	Code
United States	.us	Canada	.ca
England	.uk	Japan	.jp
Mexico	.mx	France	.fr
Iraq	.iq	Russia	.ru
Antarctica	.aq	Cuba	.cu

Basic Navigation

Let's explore how Microsoft Edge enables you to navigate the web. With some basic buttons and commands, you can move from location to location.

- **Address bar:** The address bar is where you enter the address of a web page or website.
- **Back and Forward buttons:** The Back button takes you back to previously viewed web pages while the Forward button returns you to more recently viewed web pages.
- **Refresh button:** Some web pages have content that changes frequently (such as an auction site). The Refresh button enables you to reload the page without having to type the address in the address bar again. The Refresh button replaces the Stop button once a web page has loaded.

- **Stop button:** This button stops a page from loading. If a web page is taking too long to load, clicking the Stop button will stop the loading process. This enables you to type in a new address or click the Refresh button to try loading the page again.

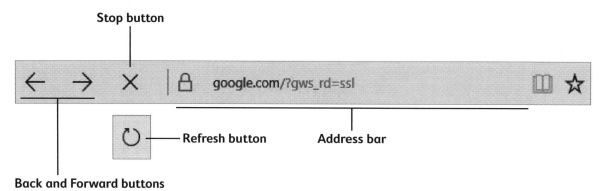

Stop button

Refresh button — Address bar

Back and Forward buttons

Hyperlinks

A **hyperlink**, or "link," is text or a picture that is linked to another page on the web. If you think of the web as a giant book, these links allow you to instantly jump from one page to another in the book.

Typically, text links will be underlined and blue in color. On occasion, you will find text links that are in a color other than blue. Picture links can look like a normal image or be designed to look like buttons.

When your mouse cursor is over a picture or text link, it will turn into a small hand with a pointing finger. When you click the mouse, you will be taken to whatever page that link points to.

Once you reach a web page or a website, you can move to other web pages on the same site or to other websites by clicking the hyperlinks.

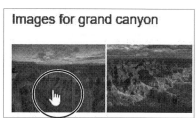

When your mouse pointer is over a link in a web page, the pointer turns into a small hand.

Tip!   Webpage, web page, and page are all used interchangeably to describe a web page on the Internet. In this book, we use the two-word form: web page.

🖰 HANDS-ON 8.1 Navigate to a Web Page

In this exercise, you will enter the address for Google News and use the Back button to navigate.

1. Start Microsoft Edge.

2. Click in the address bar.

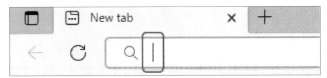

3. Type **news.google.com** as shown and tap ⌷Enter⌷.

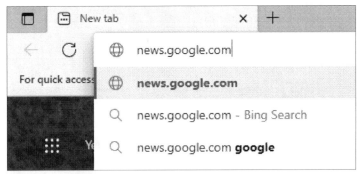

Notice that Microsoft Edge gives you a list of possible web addresses as you type. Using these can save you time when entering long addresses.

4. Use the **Back** ⌷←⌷ button to return to the Microsoft Edge start page.

. . . .

Tabbed Browsing

One of the features in most browsers is tabbed browsing. This feature enables you to have multiple web pages open at the same time. Each web page has a tab (like a recipe card), making it easy to flip through your open web pages.

This feature comes in handy when you are doing research because you can have multiple sources open at the same time and quickly jump back and forth among them by clicking the tabs. It's also a great way to scan news headlines because it enables you to have multiple newspaper websites open simultaneously.

Tip! Tabbed browsing is particularly useful when your Internet connection is running slowly; as one page is loading, you can be reading another.

The busy symbol appears while the web page is loading. Even with a high-speed connection, you may have to wait for a page to load because of congestion on the web or the popularity of a website.

This image shows Microsoft Edge with three web pages open on different tabs. The first is still loading and displays the system busy symbol.

HANDS-ON 8.2 Use Tabbed Browsing

In this exercise, you will open two web pages within Microsoft Edge.

1. Click in the address bar; type **news.google.com** and tap Enter.

2. Click the small plus button to the right of the larger tab labeled *Google News*.

A new tab is created.

3. Click in the address bar; type **cnn.com** and tap Enter.

Microsoft Edge opens the CNN web page and displays the name in the new web page tab. You should now have two tabs open.

4. Click the **Google News** tab.

You jump back to Google News.

5. Click the **CNN.com** news tab.

The browser's view switches back to CNN.

6. Click the **Google News** tab.

7. Close the Google News tab.

The Google News tab closes while the CNN tab remains displayed.

8. Close Microsoft Edge.

Printing a Web Page

Web pages can be printed if you need a paper copy. Unlike printing a document in Word, you may find that web pages don't always print the way you would expect them to. This is because web pages are designed to look good on screen, and the layout technology used to do that makes the printed-out document look slightly different. A web page also has menus, ads, and other visual tools that get printed with the document.

Sometimes a web page will have a Print button. Whenever possible, use that button, because most of the time the Print button will print a page without all the menus and other visual tools that make the web page print incorrectly.

Tip! A web page can be much longer than a standard page. Make sure to scroll to the bottom of a web page to get an idea of how long the "page" is before you print it.

HANDS-ON 8.3 Print a Web Page

In this exercise, you will go through the steps to print a web page, but you'll cancel the printing and not actually print the web page so as not to waste paper.

1. Open Microsoft Edge.

2. Type **nps.gov/grca/index.htm** in the address bar and press Enter.

3. Close any pop-up messages that appear.

4. Click the **Settings and More** (three dots) button on the right-hand side of the menu bar and choose **Print** from the menu.

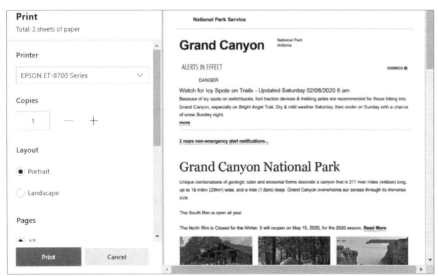

On the left side of the screen, notice that many of the page setup options are the same as those available in Word.

5. Scroll the preview up and down using the scroll bar to view the pages that will be printed.

Notice how the printed pages look nothing like the web page you are viewing.

6. Click **Cancel** at the bottom of the Print dialog box.

7. Close Microsoft Edge.

. . . .

Favorites

A **favorite** is a link to a web page that you save in your browser. A favorite makes it easy for you to return to a web page in the future. Microsoft Edge gives you the ability to store numerous addresses in its list of favorites.

When you make a website a favorite, you do not have to remember its address or accurately type it in the address bar every time you want to visit the site. You simply access it from the Favorites center.

A folder to organize favorites

Favorites (links to websites)

Tip! Not all browsers use the term "favorites." Some browsers, such as Firefox, use the term "bookmark" instead.

Ctrl + D to add a web page to your favorites

HANDS-ON 8.4 Create a Favorite

In this exercise, you will create a favorite in Microsoft Edge.

1. Open Microsoft Edge.

2. Click in the address bar; type **google.com** and tap Enter.

3. Click the **Add This Page to Favorites** button.

4. Follow these steps to name your favorite:

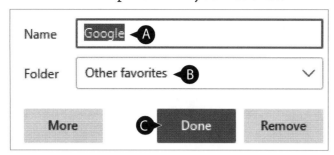

Ⓐ The default name is selected; if necessary, type **Google** to replace it. The default name may not always be descriptive enough and can be changed.

Ⓑ From the Folder menu, choose **Other Favorites**.

Ⓒ Click **Done**.

Your link to Google has been added to the Favorites center.

5. Click the **Favorites** button and then click **Other Favorites**.

Notice that your link is now in Other Favorites.

6. Close Microsoft Edge.

Favorites Bar

When enabled, the Favorites Bar displays the favorites of your choice just under the menu bar at the top of the Microsoft Edge browser window. Generally, the Favorites bar is used for favorites that you use all the time.

For example, you could put OneDrive and Outlook on your Favorites bar, making them easier to access.

Tip! The Favorites button will be a solid color (currently blue) when an address in the address bar is already in the Favorites folder.

🖱 HANDS-ON 8.5 Enable the Favorites Bar

In this exercise, you will turn on the Favorites bar and add favorites to the Favorites bar folder.

1. Start Microsoft Edge.

2. Click the **Settings and More** (three dots) button on the right side of the menu bar and choose **Settings**.

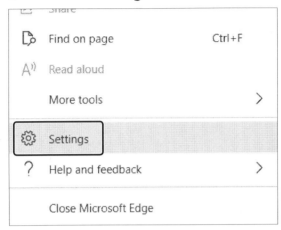

3. Click the **Appearance** option in the Settings menu at left.

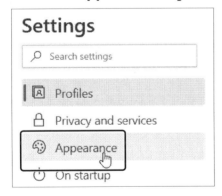

4. Set the Show Favorites Bar option to **Always**.

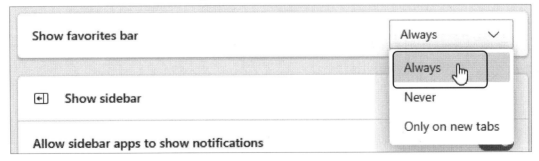

5. In the address bar, type **onedrive.com** and press ⌴Enter⌴.

6. Click the **Add This Page to Favorites** button.

7. Follow these steps to add OneDrive to the Favorites bar:

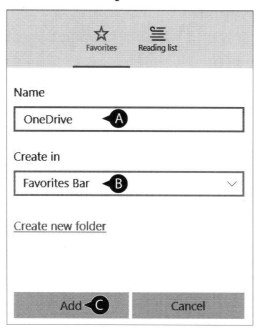

Ⓐ Change the name of the favorite to: **OneDrive**

Ⓑ Select **Favorites Bar** as the location you want the link to be created in.

Ⓒ Click **Add**.

8. Watch as the OneDrive favorite is added to the Favorites bar at the top of the Microsoft Edge browser.

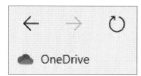

9. Repeat steps 5–8 to add **Outlook** to the Favorites bar.

10. Close Microsoft Edge.

Creating Folders in Favorites

Like you have done in Outlook, OneDrive, and Windows, you can also create folders in Favorites to organize your favorites. New folders can be created as needed when adding favorites or from the Favorites menu.

Being able to organize your Favorites is a critical feature. When you first get started, you won't have many, but as time goes on, most people end up with literally hundreds of favorites in their Favorites. Without organization, it's difficult to find a saved link when you need it again.

Tip!   It's more important to save favorites for web pages that you work hard to find than for popular websites. Popular websites are easy to find again, whereas a specific web page of information that was buried deep within a website is not so easy to find.

HANDS-ON 8.6 Create a Folder to Sort Favorites

In this exercise, you will create a folder to sort your news links into.

1. Start Microsoft Edge.

2. In the address bar, type **www.c-span.org** and tap ⎡Enter⎤.

3. Click the **Add This Page to Favorites** button.

4. In the Folder drop-down menu, select **Choose Another Folder**.

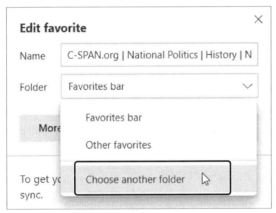

5. Click the **New Folder** button.

6. Name the folder **News** and click **Save**.

7. Choose **Favorites→Other Favorites→News**.

Verify that the C-SPAN favorite is there.

8. Close Microsoft Edge.

Removing Favorites

As desired, you can delete favorites and folders. Note that deleted favorites can be undeleted (or returned) for a very short time.

HANDS-ON 8.7 Remove a Favorite

In this exercise, you will delete a favorite from the Favorites menu.

1. Start Microsoft Edge.

2. In the address bar, type **seattletimes.com** and press Enter .

3. Add this website as a favorite in the News folder.

4. Choose **Favorites→Other Favorites→News**.

5. Right-click the **The Seattle Times** favorite and choose **Delete**.

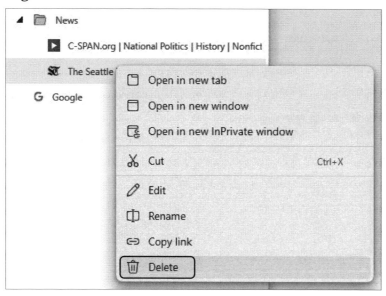

6. Close Microsoft Edge.

History

The History tab keeps a list of all the web pages you have viewed. You can go back through the history and click on any link to view that web page.

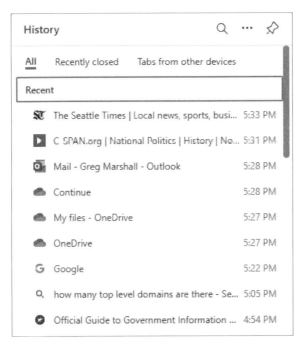

The History tab may also be cleared by using Clear Browsing Data in the More Options menu.

Downloads

The Downloads tab is a list of files you have downloaded. These are actual files that reside in the Download folder on your computer.

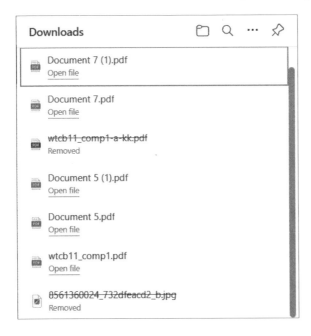

Self-Assessment

To check your knowledge of the key concepts introduced in this chapter, complete this Self-Assessment quiz.

1. Only seven domains are available for use worldwide.   **true**   **false**

2. A router enables only a single computer to connect to a high-speed Internet connection.   **true**   **false**

3. Hyperlinks are links to other pages on the web.   **true**   **false**

4. A favorite is a link to a web page saved in your web browser for later.   **true**   **false**

5. The Favorites bar is always displayed on the screen.   **true**   **false**

6. The feature in Microsoft Edge that lets you open multiple web pages in the same window is called tabbed browsing.   **true**   **false**

7. Which piece of equipment is used to connect multiple computers to an Internet connection?

   A. Modem

   B. Phone line

   C. Router

   D. Network

8. Besides Microsoft Edge, another web browser is _____.

   A. Internet Explorer

   B. Chrome

   C. Yahoo

   D. Both A and B

⬡ Skill Builders

SKILL BUILDER 8.1 Create a Favorite

In this exercise, you will create favorites for some popular news sites.

1. Start Microsoft Edge.

2. In the address bar type **cnn.com** and press ⎡Enter⎤.

3. Click the **Add This Page to Favorites** button and save the link to the **Other Favorites** folder.

4. Create favorites for nytimes.com and latimes.com.

5. Open the Other Favorites folder and verify that the three new favorites are there.

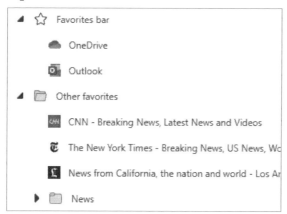

6. Close Microsoft Edge.

SKILL BUILDER 8.2 Drag Favorites to Folders

In this exercise, you will organize your news favorites by dragging them into the News folder.

1. Start Microsoft Edge.

2. Click the **Other Favorites** button at the top of the screen.

3. Drag the **New York Times** favorite over the **News** folder and release.

Notice how the entire link is moved by the mouse and placed on top of the News folder.

4. Drag the **Los Angeles Times** favorite into the **News** folder.

5. Verify that your links are now in the News folder.

6. Close Microsoft Edge.

··

SKILL BUILDER 8.3 Move Favorites and Folders

Favorites and folders can be repositioned to better organize your favorites list. In this exercise, you will create a new folder and position it in the Favorites Bar folder.

1. Open Microsoft Edge and then click the **Other Favorites** button.

2. Right-click the **News** folder and click **Add Folder** on the menu that appears.

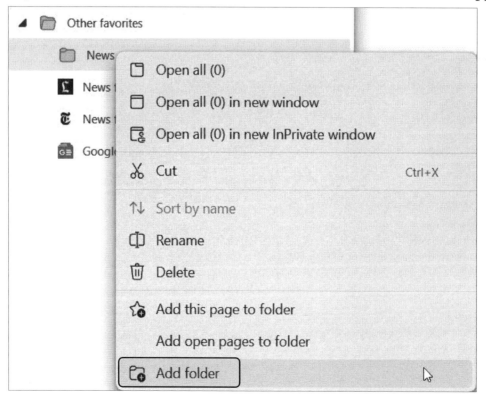

3. Name the new folder **Project Research** and press Enter.

4. Drag the **Project Research** folder under the **News** folder and release.

   Notice how the other favorites and folders attempt to make room for the folder as you drag across them.

5. Move the **News** folder under the **Project Research** folder if it isn't already there.

6. Close Microsoft Edge.

· ·

SKILL BUILDER 8.4 Download Chrome

You have your choice of many different browsers, and you don't have to use the browser that comes with your computer. In this exercise, you will download Google's Chrome browser and install it on your home computer.

1. Open Microsoft Edge.

2. Type **google.com/chrome** in the address bar and tap Enter.

   This will take you to the download page for Chrome.

3. Click **Download Chrome** (currently in the middle of the page).

4. Click **Accept and Install**.

   After a few minutes, the Chrome setup program will finish downloading.

5. Click **Open File** on the menu that appears.

6. Click **Yes** when asked if you want to allow the app to make changes to your PC.

   It will take a few minutes for Chrome to be installed. A dialog box in the middle of the screen will keep you informed of where you are in the process. After installation, Chrome will automatically open.

7. Look for Google Chrome on your Start menu under "G."

Spend some time using Chrome. Many of the things you learned about Microsoft Edge in this chapter also apply to Chrome.

8. Close Microsoft Edge.

. . . .

CHAPTER 9

Researching on the Internet

LEARNING OBJECTIVES

- Use Google to perform a basic search
- Use Google to search for images
- Protect yourself from web threats
- Complete a complicated search

The Internet is a powerful tool for finding information. Access to information grows and expands at an unfathomable pace that was unthinkable just a generation ago. In this chapter, you will explore how to search the Internet for various types of information and learn how to protect yourself and your computer against web threats.

Learning Resources: **boostyourskills.lablearning.com**

📂 Case Study: Web Research

Patrick is still planning his trip to the Grand Canyon. Now that he has his trip basics set, Patrick wants to know more information about the canyon and the area around it. His friend Clarice suggests he use the Google search engine at google.com.

As Patrick starts typing in some search words, he is surprised that Google provides some potential search "strings" as he types. He clicks on a search string titled "grand canyon information and facts," and the search engine returns a list of websites and pages with information and facts about the Grand Canyon.

Looking through the results, Patrick finds a page from the National Parks, which he loves! He clicks the link and spends some time learning facts about the Grand Canyon and its history.

Performing a Basic Web Search

Finding information on the web is easy if you know where the information is located and you have a web address (URL) already. When you don't know its location, finding information can be more difficult. Luckily, there are tools called **search engines** that can help you find the information you want from the millions of pages that make up the web.

Search engines are specialized websites that help you find and sort information on the web. Think of a search engine as your own personal web librarian.

How Search Engines Work

Search engines, such as Google, index the web in a way that is similar to how Windows indexes the information on your computer and then uses that index when you use the Search command in a folder window.

Google indexes the web using a vast network of computers around the world that index, or "crawl," the web every few days. When you perform a search, the search engine creates a list of the most relevant web pages it has indexed based on your search words.

Basic Search Techniques

When you search for information on the web using a search engine, it's important to choose the correct words to describe an item. Here are some tips to help you with your searches:

- **Pick a few keywords to describe your search item:** In most cases, three or four words should be enough.
- **Be specific:** If you are interested in books about Windows, using "computer books" to search will display millions of possible web pages, or "hits," but the list will be too broad. You can narrow your search with more specific words, such as "Windows 11 books." This will bring up a shorter list of web pages that are more relevant.
- **Spell your search words correctly:** Misspelled words will generate a list, but it is not likely to be useful.
- **Keep trying:** If you are not finding what you are looking for, add and remove words from your search, and try different words. Even on the web, some subjects can be difficult to find information on. For example, if you are trying to find information on stabilizing riverbanks, "stabilize" and "bank" would be difficult words to use in a search, because you would tend to get mostly financial news related to banking issues. You could try using words such as "stream," "restoration," or "erosion" with the word "river." Sometimes when searching, the quickest way to finding an answer is not the most obvious.

 HANDS-ON 9.1 Search with Google

In this exercise, you will perform a basic search using Google. Because the content of the Internet can change rapidly, the information in your search may be slightly different from what is shown on the screen.

1. Start Microsoft Edge.

2. Type **google.com** in the address bar and tap ⌶Enter⌶.

   ← ⟳ G google.com

   The Google search engine web page appears. Like many search engines, Google works best when you enter three or four words that describe what you are looking for. In this example, you will be looking for information on skiing at Mount Baker.

3. Type the word **mountain** in the Search box.

   As you type, Google will try to guess what you are searching for and make suggestions for you to select from.

4. Tap Enter .

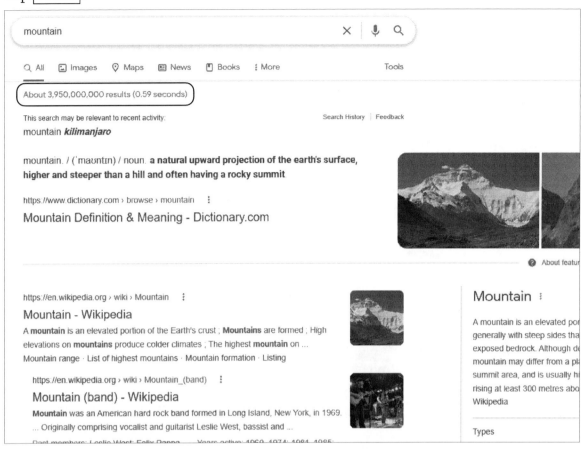

If you don't put enough information into your search, you won't end up with the information you are looking for. The word mountain *is not specific enough to get you the information you want. Notice the number of pages found at the top of the search results. (The number of results found on your computer may differ.)*

Narrow the Search

Rather than tediously going through search result pages until you see if you can find one about Mount Baker, add some keywords to narrow the search.

5. In the Search box, type **baker** and **skiing** after *mountain* and then tap Enter .

You will notice that by adding just a couple more search terms, the top hits are related to the subject you are looking for.

6. Click the **Mt. Baker Ski Area : Home** link.

   This will take you to the actual website where information about skiing at Mount Baker can be found.

7. Close Microsoft Edge.

. . . .

Improving Your Search Results

Modern searching is pretty straightforward. Search engines are now smart enough that they can usually tell what you are searching for and display the correct search results, but keep the following points in mind to help ensure this is the case:

- **Word order matters:** The first few words in your search should be the main descriptive words for what you are looking for. Other words in your search support these first few words.

- **Type in lowercase:** Always search using lowercase text. If you capitalize words, a search engine looks only for web pages where words are capitalized. If you don't capitalize, it will look for words of either case.

- **Spelling counts!** If you spell search words wrong, it will search for those wrongly spelled words. Amazingly you will still find results, just not the results you were expecting. Sometimes the search engine will suggest possible correct spellings to improve your search.

- **Use a minus sign:** If you put a minus sign before a word, the search engine will not show any page that has that word in it. For example, if I am searching for pages on Mount Baker and all I see are pages on skiing, I could use *–skiing* to remove all those ski pages.

Warning! Careful! The minus sign is a clumsy tool. You could end up removing pages with the information you need just because they also reference that particular word you want removed.

- **Type a question:** Modern search engines can understand when you type your search as a complete sentence. Sometimes typing a complete sentence is easier than coming up with primary words.

The World of Search Engines

In this chapter, Google is used to illustrate navigation and search concepts, but it is just one of the many search engines you can use. The web has millions of pages stored on millions of connected computers scattered across the globe, so no single search engine will always provide the information that you're looking for.

Because of the way search engines filter the information shown, you can get different results from using the same search words on different search engines. It is like different chefs cooking the same recipe; each has a "secret ingredient" that gives his or her results a distinct flavor.

Besides Google (google.com), other popular search engines include Yahoo! (yahoo.com), Bing from Microsoft (bing.com), and DuckDuckGo (duckduckgo.com).

Many search engines also have specialized searches for specific types of information. Google, for example, has the ability to search just images or just news-related websites.

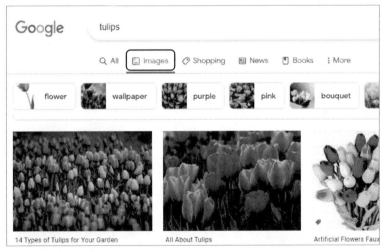

Google allows many types of searches, including one for images.

Despite all of the capabilities these search engines have to index the web, some information is still not within their reach. Many sites that generate their own content (such as newspapers, magazines, and archive sites) do not allow outside search engines to index their sites. They use search engines built into their websites that are designed specifically to search their data. To access the data from this type of site, you would need to go directly to one. This is helpful to know if you're not finding the information you seek with search engines.

The Hidden Web

Only a small fraction of the Internet is indexed by search engines. Much of what is on the Internet is hidden away and needs to be found by other methods. These hidden sites usually require registration and/or payment to use. For example, many schools subscribe to ProQuest, which is a database of research papers and articles perfect for researching information for your own papers. ProQuest is Internet based but not searchable from a search engine.

Luckily your school's library has likely already purchased access to many of these databases of information on the Internet.

Difficult Searches

Most searches are fairly easy. Search engines have gotten powerful enough to interpret your search needs from just a few entered words. However, you will occasionally run into a search that just won't work.

When you're having trouble finding the information you need, consider the suggestions outlined in the following table:

STEPS TO SOLVING A DIFFICULT SEARCH	
Try...	**Reason...**
Put in two or three words that describe what you are looking for (spelled correctly!).	The first few words are the primary triggers for the search engine.
Add a couple more words to narrow the search.	More descriptive words give the search engine more to work with.
Change the word order of your search.	Different primary words will produce a different search result.
Use a different search engine.	Search engines all work in slightly different ways. Using a different search engine may produce a different result.
Search a news, reference, or research site.	Not all information is scanned by search engines. Many sites want you to come and visit them "in person."
Ask a librarian.	Many libraries have a reference librarian who is an expert searcher. They can help you with a difficult search.

Tip! Libraries are no longer just about books. Librarians are gatekeepers and expert resources on information available on the Internet.

Searching for Images

Many search engines, including Google, allow you to search specifically for images. This can be useful, say, when you need images for your research papers and projects.

Tip! Just because a search engine shows you an image, it doesn't always mean you have the right to use the image. Copyright laws apply to objects you find while searching. Do your own research regarding copyright laws, and be aware that following them is your responsibility.

HANDS-ON 9.2 Do a Google Image Search

In this exercise, you will use Google to find images of the Grand Canyon.

1. Open Microsoft Edge and go to: **google.com**

2. Type **grand canyon** in the Search box and press Enter.

3. Click **Images** at the top of the search list.

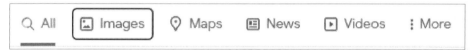

4. Scroll through the images. Note the variety, as well as how the images are sorted by subject at the top of the page.

5. In the search box, add the word **lightning** to the end of your search and press Enter.

   Adding a third search word to your image search narrows the search down to just pictures with lightning in them.

6. Click the first picture.

Notice that when you click the picture you get related images, a link to visit the page that hosts the picture, and a link for viewing the image at its original size. Because images are being added to the Internet daily, the images in your search may be slightly different from those shown here.

7. Close Microsoft Edge.

Defending Yourself from Web Threats

The World Wide Web is a powerful tool that gives you access to information and products. Unfortunately, it also can allow threats, such as computer **viruses**, to access your computer. Once your computer is connected to the Internet, you need to be aware of the threats to it and how to protect against them.

Threats While Surfing

The browser and web pages can be a source of threats to your computer. Web pages can track information using small pieces of code called **cookies**. Not all cookies are bad, but tracking does allow information on you to be kept.

Other websites will try to get you to click on links that will download programs to your computer. This software will run in the background and try to steal passwords, access credit card information, and more.

Advertising on some sites will try to convince you that your machine needs to be fixed or updated and attempt to get you to sign-up for expensive services you don't need.

Protection Software

The first line of protection for your computer is software that monitors and repels or fixes the damage done by various web threats. With the proper software installed on your computer, you will have very few problems when surfing the Internet.

Firewall Software

Firewall software is one way to protect your computer from various Internet threats. A firewall acts much like the outer defensive wall on a medieval castle.

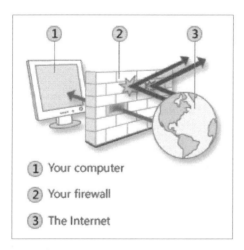

1 Your computer

2 Your firewall

3 The Internet

Windows comes with a built-in firewall. The firewall checks all data coming into the computer and blocks any data (based on rules programmed into the firewall) that is deemed a threat. Many retail firewalls provide additional features like automatic updates, automatic scanning for viruses, and email scanning. Many firewall programs come in a suite that also includes antivirus and other software designed to protect your computer.

Antivirus Software

Computer viruses are small programs designed to disrupt your computer. They can be picked up from websites, email, and various types of documents. Some viruses are irritating, others destroy files, and the worst try to steal personal information.

Antivirus software works by looking for signs (or "signatures") of viruses in all data coming into the computer and in any files being used by the computer. Some antivirus software also watches the computer for strange activity that may be a sign of a virus infection.

Using Social Media Sites Safely

Social media sites are websites where people and/or businesses with mutual interests are linked in order to communicate. Communications can take many forms: written posts, game play, picture and video sharing, news sharing, and online discussions. Visitors to a site are often encouraged to share comments or join in discussions about information posted. Social sites encourage and facilitate two-way communication.

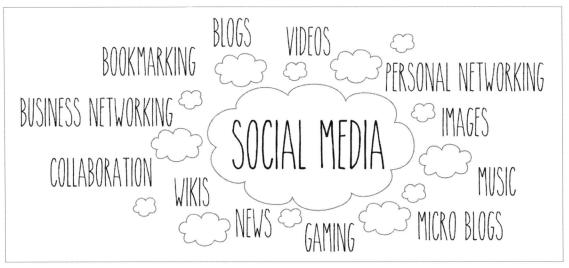

Social media sites facilitate two-way communication in many ways.

A social media site may have a narrow or a broad focus. YouTube is a site primarily used to share videos. Two popular sites, Facebook and Pinterest, are primarily social networking sites, but they also facilitate picture, video, and music sharing. Blogger provides personal and business blogs for sharing written posts that can include pictures, videos, comments, and discussions. Sites like LinkedIn specifically target businesses, whereas Yelp! targets people who want to share recommendations for services like restaurants.

With any Internet activity, you have to protect your privacy and be vigilant about avoiding scams and the inappropriate use of your personal information. As you link yourself with others online, keep the following information in mind:

- Assume that any information you share on the Internet may stay there *forever*. You must be careful about what you say and be very selective with the pictures and videos you post. The information you post can resurface many years later, and you never know who will see it. The information could become personally embarrassing or adversely affect things like job opportunities.
- Never share your login and password information with anyone.

- Always be wary of "friends" you make online. Your trust should be given carefully to online friends. Scams can happen when online contacts become your friends to gather personal information. Others may take advantage of your network to spread misinformation.

Antispyware

Spyware usually takes the form of cookies and other bits of software that get installed when you visit a website. These bits can gather and store information and be sent to the host, who can then sell your information. Antispyware scans your machine and removes these cookies and software bits, reducing the threat they pose.

Updating Your Software

Most new computers come with antivirus software installed as a free trial, but at some point you will need to pay for a subscription that keeps it updated. Antivirus software needs to be updated regularly because new viruses are constantly being created. Without updates, your antivirus software will slowly become less effective.

Steps You Can Take

Antivirus and antispyware software will do much of the heavy lifting when it comes to protecting you against web threats, but there are a few simple things you can do to minimize web threats even more and make your Internet experiences safer and a lot more fun!

SAFETY STEPS	
Action	**Reason**
Keep software updated.	Manufacturers update software frequently to fix problems that might cause security issues.
Change passwords frequently.	This makes any passwords that have been exposed on the Internet useless.
Reboot your computer or device every few days.	We tend to leave our PCs and devices on for days and weeks. Rebooting clears any malicious code from memory.
Be aware.	Use the Internet with a bit of caution. Be cautious of untrusted sites, sites with lots of ads, and strange promises.

Self-Assessment

To check your knowledge of the key concepts introduced in this chapter, complete this Self-Assessment quiz.

1. Search engines index the web.   **true   false**

2. Google indexes everything on the Internet.   **true   false**

3. Search engines search for text only.   **true   false**

4. You may freely use images you find on the web.   **true   false**

5. Once antivirus software is installed, your computer is protected from most threats—if updated regularly.   **true   false**

6. Passwords should never be changed as it is hard to remember new ones.   **true   false**

7. Which is NOT a piece of protection software for your computer?

   A. Firewall

   B. Antivirus

   C. Antispyware

   D. eFence

8. When using a search engine, it's best to enter _____.

   A. dozens of words describing what you are looking for

   B. words to vaguely describe what you're looking for to make sure you cover all potential search areas

   C. one word to describe what you're looking for

   D. a few keywords to describe what you're looking for

9. Which statement is NOT true?

   A. Passwords should be changed frequently.

   B. Images and comments posted online eventually get deleted.

   C. Never share your login and password with anyone online.

   D. Antivirus software needs to be updated on a regular basis to stay effective.

 # Skill Builders

SKILL BUILDER 9.1 **Search for Copyright-Safe Images**

Google enables you to search for images that have copyrights that allow for reuse. (You are still responsible for ensuring that images you use for certain purposes are copyright free or in the public domain.) In this exercise, you will use a Google Images search to find a copyright-safe image of the Grand Tetons.

1. Start Microsoft Edge and go to: **google.com**

2. In the search box, type **tetons** and press Enter .

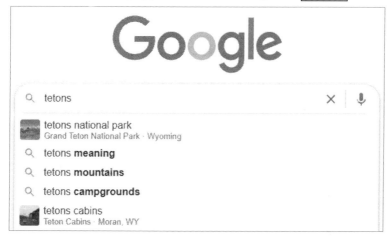

Notice that as you type, Google immediately starts showing relevant information.

3. Click **Images** at the top of the search page.

4. Click **Tools**.

Since we are in Images, the image tools appear (Size, Color, Type, etc.).

5. Click **Usage Rights** and then choose **Creative Commons Licenses**.

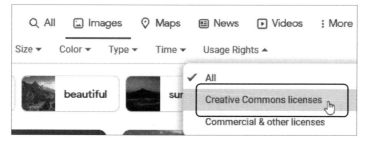

Creative Commons Licenses is for use in school papers or any activity that you don't make money from. Notice the screen shows a different collection of images.

SKILL BUILDER 9.2 Save an Image

In this exercise, you will download an image to your computer.

Before You Begin: Make sure your USB flash drive is plugged in.

1. Click any image of the Grand Teton.

   Google brings up a bigger version of the image and more options.

2. Hover over the image with your mouse pointer. If your mouse pointer shows a plus sign, click.

   The plus sign means the image is too large for the screen. Clicking shows you the actual size, even if the image is bigger than the screen. Clicking again makes the image fit on the screen.

3. Right-click the image and choose **Save Image As**.

4. Choose your **USB flash drive** and click **Save**.

   A copy of the picture is now saved on your USB flash drive.

5. Close Microsoft Edge.

SKILL BUILDER 9.3 Clear Browsing Data

As you use you use the Internet, your browser saves copies of all the information you have viewed. Cookies from the various websites you have visited build up, and the sum total of this information not only becomes a security issue, it slows down the browser. In this exercise, you will clear your browsing data from Microsoft Edge.

1. Start Microsoft Edge.

2. Click **Settings**.

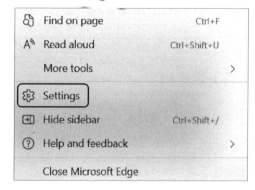

3. Choose **Privacy, Search and Services** in the Settings menu.

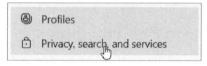

4. Under *Clear Browsing Data* click **Choose What to Clear**.

5. Set the Time Range option to **All Time**, ensure the boxes for the top four options are checked, and then click **Clear Now**.

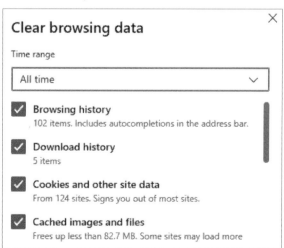

The other three items are not as important to clear and might impact your ease of use of the browser if cleared. Clearing data may take a minute as there may be hundreds of small files to delete.

6. While the data is clearing, you will see a Clear Browsing Data message and a graphic of a rotating circle.

When the process is complete, the message and graphic will disappear.

7. Close Microsoft Edge.

SKILL BUILDER 9.4 **Search for News**

Google enables you to search specifically for news articles on the Internet. In this exercise, you will use Google to search for current news articles on global warming.

1. If necessary, start Microsoft Edge and go to: **google.com**

2. Type **global warming** into the search box and press Enter.

3. Click **News** on the menu bar.

Notice that all the results are now news stories from various news sources.

4. Click **Tools**.

Notice that a secondary toolbar appears with tools related to the news.

5. Choose **Sorted by Relevance→Sorted by Date**.

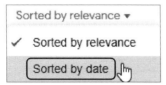

The search results are now sorted by date order with the newest being on top. As you like, take some time to read a few of the articles.

6. Close Microsoft Edge.

CHAPTER 10

Using Settings and Help

LEARNING OBJECTIVES

- Search your computer using the new Search program

- Change the screen resolution and Desktop background

- Change the power options

- Update Windows 11

Your Windows computer came with a certain look and with the features set to work in a certain way. These settings are not always optimal for the way you like to work. Likewise, it can be difficult to find information and settings on your computer, as Windows has become very complex and has lots of customization options. In this chapter, you will customize the look and feel of your computer and use the new Search feature to search your computer and the Internet for information. You will also learn about updating Windows to keep the system and its various features working at their maximum efficiency.

Learning Resources: **boostyourskills.lablearning.com**

📁 Case Study: Power Options

Dan is frustrated. His new PC laptop is running really slowly—even more slowly than the old laptop that he just replaced. The battery isn't the problem, as he always plugs his laptop into the wall when he is using it.

Dan decides to ask his son Greg, a technologist, about it. Greg has him go into the System command under Settings and look for the Additional Power Settings. Greg tells him that most new PCs and laptops have the power setting set to Balanced, which extends battery life but *really* slows down the computer. He explains that changing to High Performance makes your computer a lot faster and should be the setting you use when plugged into the wall.

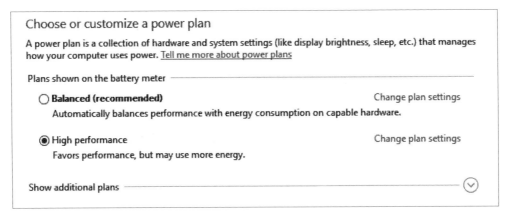

Dan makes the change and is amazed by how much faster his computer runs. Now Dan switches between High Performance and Balanced, depending on whether he is plugged into a power source or running on his battery.

Searching Windows and the Web

Windows has a robust search feature that's accessible right from the taskbar. Using this Search box, you can scan for items such as files, folders, and apps on your computer and on the web (using the Bing search engine).

Search icon

Search results are organized into multiple sections including Best Match, **Settings**, Apps, Docs, Email, and Web. The following illustration shows the results of a search for *settings*:

Other search hits are organized on these tabs.

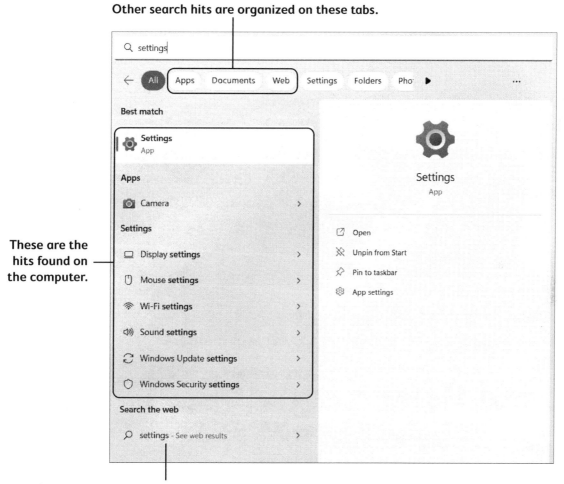

These are the hits found on the computer.

Typing "settings" in the Search box brings up a variety of hits.

🖱 HANDS-ON 10.1 Perform a Basic Search

In this exercise, you will do a basic search using the Search box.

1. Click in the **Search** button on the tasbkar.
   Ignore any messages that appear.

2. Type: `settings`
   Notice that as you type in your search words, the search starts to bring up possible answers.

3. Click **Settings** under *Best Match* to open the Settings window.
   The Settings app is opened. You'll look more closely at this app later in the chapter. For now, you will close it.

4. Close the Settings app.

. . . .

Choosing a Search Link to the Internet

When you select an Internet link from the Search pane, you are actually triggering an additional search using your default browser and the Bing search engine. For example, a search for "research help" brings up several hits under the Web settings. Clicking the "research helper" hit opens Microsoft Edge, and Bing searches for the term. The results may not be what you are looking for, in which case you may need to refine the search using the skills learned in Chapter 9, "Researching on the Internet."

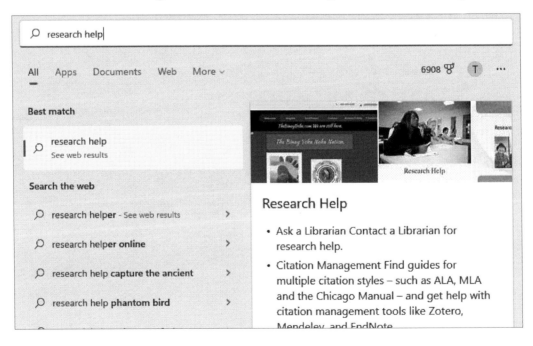

HANDS-ON 10.2 Use Windows to Search the Web

In this exercise, you will use the Search box to find help on the web.

1. Click in the **Search** box and type: `research help`

   Notice that as you type, Windows Search is already looking for the best answer.

2. Click **Research Help** under Best Match.

   Best Match will show the best result no matter what type of result it is. In this case, it is a web search.

   Watch as your web browser is started and Bing searches the web.

3. Close Microsoft Edge.

. . . .

Getting Help

You can use the Search box to find help for questions you may have about Windows. Or, if you're looking for a particular app on your PC, entering its name in the Search box will usually locate it. For help with an app, you can enter *help* followed by the name of the app or procedure.

HANDS-ON 10.3 Search for Help

In this exercise, you will use the Search box to get help for File Explorer.

1. In the Search box, type: `help with file explorer`

2. Under *Best Match*, click the **Help with File Explorer** link.

   Notice your browser opens to the Bing search engine. The results are based on the text you typed in.

3. In the Bing search box, add `in windows 11` to the end of your search string and tap [Enter].

   The search results are now focused on Windows 11.

4. Close Microsoft Edge.

. . . .

Using Settings

Settings is a very important area in Windows. It provides access to most of the programs and features necessary to change the screen appearance and the way things work in Windows.

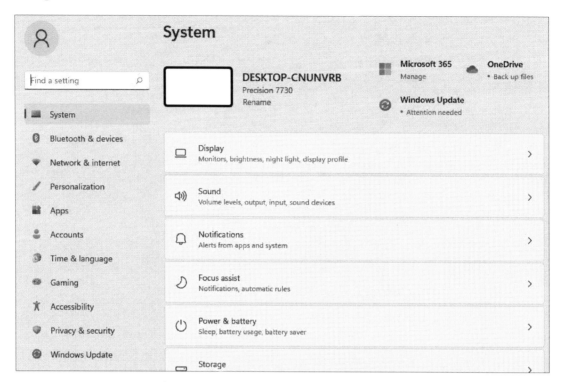

Settings are organized into categories, such as Display, Sound, and Notifications. Some categories depend on your PC, other equipment, and installed software. To access the settings within a category, you can click an item or enter a search term.

Working with Web-Based Simulations

Some of the exercises in this chapter have you work with settings that you may not be able to change on a public computer or that could otherwise be problematic if completed "live." To ensure the best learning environment for you, these exercises are available as web-based simulations (WebSims).

HANDS-ON 10.4 Change the Time and Date in the Control Panel

 In this exercise, you will check that the automatic date and time settings are turned on using a category search and a word search in Settings. This exercise runs as a WebSim.

1. Launch Microsoft Edge and go to: **boostyourskills.lablearning.com**

2. Click the **View Resources** button under the picture of your book and then click the **Unit 3** tab.

3. Click **Chapter 10** and click **Hands-On 10.4**.

   You will complete the exercise in the simulation. At the end of the simulation, return to the main course page and leave your web browser open.

. . . .

Settings Versus the Control Panel

In some previous versions of Windows, the Control Panel was the main way to access the controls that change the way your computer looks and works. Windows now promotes the Settings app, which you have just used and that offers an easier way to access even more controls.

The Control Panel is still available as of this writing. In fact, you will find that Settings opens it in a new window when you access advanced settings and controls. There are fewer and fewer settings in the Control Panel, as Microsoft continues to migrate the options to the Settings app.

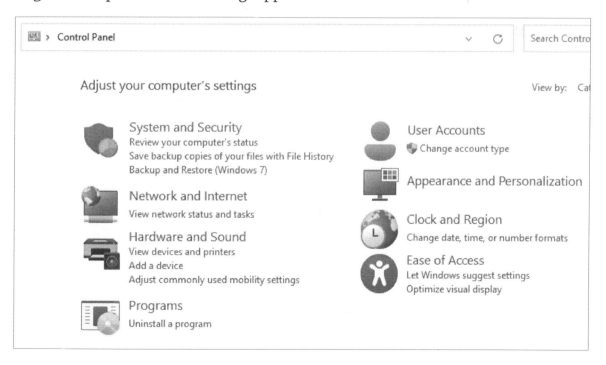

Controlling the Screen

One of the many customizations you can make in Windows is to change the resolution of your monitor. Resolution changes the visual appearance of the images on the screen, making objects more or less crisp, or larger or smaller.

Screen Resolution Settings

The digital images you see on your monitor are made up of tiny colored squares called pixels (picture elements). The resolution setting of a monitor establishes how many pixels are displayed horizontally and vertically. A screen setting of 1,024 x 768 pixels is considered low resolution. The pixels are large and may make images have jagged edges. A higher resolution setting like 1920 x 1080 displays more pixels in the same space, so the pixels are smaller. The results are the following:

- Smaller pixels can display finer lines, so images and text look sharper.
- Smaller pixels create smaller images and text, allowing more images and text to fit on the screen.
- Smaller text will be sharper but may be harder to read.

BEHIND THE SCREEN

LED Monitors and Aspect Ratios

To take advantage of Windows' marvelous graphics capabilities, people are more often than not opting to buy flat-panel LED (light emitting diode) monitors for their new computers. Because of their trim size and lighter weight, they take up less room on your desktop and are easier to set up and move around than older-style monitors. They are also available in a variety of sizes and shapes.

LED Panels and Wide Screens

Older-style CRT (cathode ray tube) monitors had one screen shape but different diagonal measurements—14-inch, 15-inch, 17-inch, 19-inch, 20-inch, and so on. LED panels vary in both size and shape. The viewable screen is measured diagonally to determine LED size (note that CRT sizing often includes the case).

Different Resolutions, Different Aspect Ratios

LCD screens are assembled with a fixed number of liquid crystals horizontally and vertically (referred to as their native resolution). Although screens have a native resolution, the resolution or number of pixels displayed horizontally and vertically can be changed (see the Changing Monitor Resolution table on the next page). Changing the resolution also may change the **aspect ratio** of the screen. If you change to a resolution setting with fewer pixels than the native resolution, the unused screen pixels may appear as black bands above and below the image (letterbox format).

With some resolution settings, monitors may display in letterbox format.

Standard and Widescreen Aspect Ratios

Common aspect ratios for LCD panels

CRT screens (older computer monitors and non-HD TVs) have an aspect ratio of 4:3 (for every four pixels displayed horizontally, three pixels are displayed vertically). LCD screens are available in several aspect ratios, including 4:3. LCD screens with aspect ratios of 15:9, 16:9, or 16:10 would be called *widescreen*. When you adjust the screen resolution, you may also be changing the aspect ratio. Manufacturers continue to make larger screens with higher resolutions and various aspect ratios.

Using the Settings, you can change the screen resolution on most monitors from as low as 800 × 600 to 1920 × 1080 or higher.

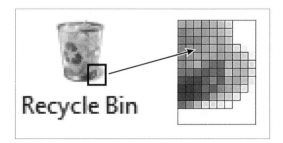

When the Recycle Bin icon is magnified several hundred percent, you can see that it is made up of square pixels of different shades and colors.

CHANGING MONITOR RESOLUTION

Task	Procedure
Locate the Display Resolution box	■ Choose Start→Settings. ■ From the System category, choose Display.
Change the resolution	■ Click the Resolution drop-down menu and choose the desired resolution. ■ The screen may go dark momentarily and then return with the new resolution (if the resolution is higher, items on the screen look smaller, and if the settings are lower, the items look larger). ■ Click Keep Changes to accept or Revert to cancel. ■ If you see a warning saying "Resolution Setting Not Supported," *do not* click any buttons. Let the program revert to the original resolution and then try a different resolution.

Changing the Background Image

The **background** (also called the wallpaper) of the Desktop can be personalized to show a solid color or your favorite image. Computer manufacturers often place their logos on the background or use a design or color that you don't care for, but it's easy and fun to change the background color or image. If you own a digital camera, you have access to an endless supply of possible images of friends, relatives, pets, or your favorite places.

Tip! Avoid images that are cluttered or comprised of colors that make it difficult to see your Desktop icons.

CHANGING THE DESKTOP BACKGROUND

Task	Procedure
Change the background	■ Choose Start→Settings. ■ From the Personalization category, choose Background. ■ Click the Background drop-down menu button and choose Picture, Solid Color, or Slideshow. ■ Picture: Choose from the menu of recent images or click Browse to search your PC. Then, pick an option from the Choose a Fit menu. ■ Solid Color: Select an option from the menu of colors. ■ Slideshow: Click Browse to choose the images to include in the slideshow. Also choose options to set the slideshow time and fit.

Note! In Skill Builder 10.2, you will change the Desktop background on your computer.

Power Options

Power is life when using a laptop or device. With a few preference changes, you can dramatically extend the length of time your laptop can run on batteries. Unfortunately, many of these preferences also slow down your computer or degrade your user experience slightly, so take care when using them.

When your computer is plugged into an outlet, you want to maximize the speed of the system over saving battery power. And when using battery power, you want that power to last as long as possible.

Battery Saver

The Battery Saver setting activates when your battery goes below a 20% charge. Note that Battery Saver makes various changes to your laptop and software, including:

- Slowing the speed at which your processor, hard drive, and other hardware work
- Dimming the screen (a bright screen takes more power)
- Limiting the activity of background apps, which keeps programs from updating and receiving data (for example, your email app doesn't keep checking for mail unless it is the active app)

When you hover your mouse pointer over the battery symbol in the system tray, it tells you how much battery life you have left and whether the battery is charging or not.

You can adjust the settings of the Battery Saver to set when it activates, which programs can continue to run in the background, and more.

Power and Sleep

When Windows detects inactivity, it can turn off the screen after a set amount of time has passed. The screen reactivates after Windows detects a keystroke or mouse movement. This can save a lot of power if you walk away from your laptop to do something else.

You can also set when the laptop goes to sleep. Sleep mode reduces all hardware to a minimal power state, turns off the monitor, and stops all app processes. In this mode, your laptop has the longest battery life possible. When a keystroke is detected or the mouse is moved, the laptop "wakes up" from Sleep. It can take your laptop 30 seconds or more to come out of Sleep mode.

Tip! Some laptops have a problem coming out of Sleep mode, depending on the hardware and software installed. If your laptop never seems to "wake up," you may want to turn this feature off.

HANDS-ON 10.5 Change Power and Battery Options

In this exercise, you will set the power and battery options of a typical laptop.
Before You Begin: The online resources should still be open in your web browser. If not, launch Microsoft Edge and go there now.

1. In the Chapter 10 section, click **Hands-On 10.5**.

2. Complete this exercise in the simulation.
   Leave your web browser open.

· ·

Additional Power Settings

Many of the additional power settings available have to do with laptops. With these settings you can control what the Power button does, what happens when you close the lid to your computer, and whether you need to reenter a password when your laptop comes out of Sleep mode.

You can also choose and customize power plans. Power plans let you choose between battery life and performance. By default, your PC will have three plans: Power Saver, which maximizes battery life; Balanced, which balances between battery and performance; and High Performance, which maximizes the speed of your computer.

Note! You should check your power-plan settings, even on a desktop PC. Many desktops come set to Balanced instead of High Performance, which means you are not running at the fastest setting your desktop is capable of.

HANDS-ON 10.6 Change the Power Plan

In this exercise, you will change the power plan on a PC. Your web browser should still be open.

1. In the Chapter 10 section, click **Hands-On 10.6**.

2. Complete this exercise in the simulation.
   Leave your web browser open.

Windows Update

Windows is a complex operating system with many components. From time to time, protection against security threats, corrections to errors in the programming, or new features and improvements will be made available as updates. Windows checks for updates roughly once per day. It will also check for updates for other Microsoft products installed on the PC if that option is selected. Your PC automatically installs updates and reboots, if needed. The automatic reboot can be set to a manual reboot in the Settings.

Note! The second Tuesday of every month is known as *patch Tuesday*. Microsoft and other companies release noncritical software updates on that day.

HANDS-ON 10.7 Set Update Options

In this exercise, you will set the options for Windows Update.

1. In the Chapter 10 section, click **Hands-On 10.7**.

2. Complete this exercise in the simulation.
   Leave your web browser open.

The Trend Toward Automatic Updates

As software has become more complicated, automatic updates have become a common software feature. At the same time, more people have access to high-speed Internet which makes it easier for developers to send updates electronically.

Before the web, people rarely got updates for their software. They often had to live with any flaws or problems in the software until the next version was available for sale. On occasion, when a flaw was bad enough to make the software unusable, a company might mail registered users a floppy disk or CD with corrections or a corrected version of the program. This happened rarely because it was very expensive for the companies, but the web has changed that.

Companies now can post updates on their websites or, better yet, provide automatic updating built into their programs. When automatic updating detects an Internet connection, a program can "call home" and check for updates that add new or improved features, or patches to fix problems. These update files are then automatically transferred to your computer. They either will be automatically installed, or you will be prompted to install them.

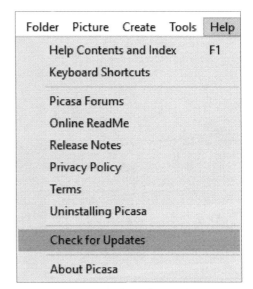

Many programs that do not have automatic updates allow you to manually check for them. This is generally done by looking for the update command on the Help menu.

Although automatic updates can be convenient, they can also be annoying when they interrupt you too often while you are trying to work. Programs with automatic update procedures may enable you to set how frequently and at what time of the day they look for updates. You may also be given choices regarding how automatic or manual the process will be.

The Store

The Store enables you to download apps to your Windows computer in much the same way as you download apps to your phone. This simplifies the process of purchasing and installing new software.

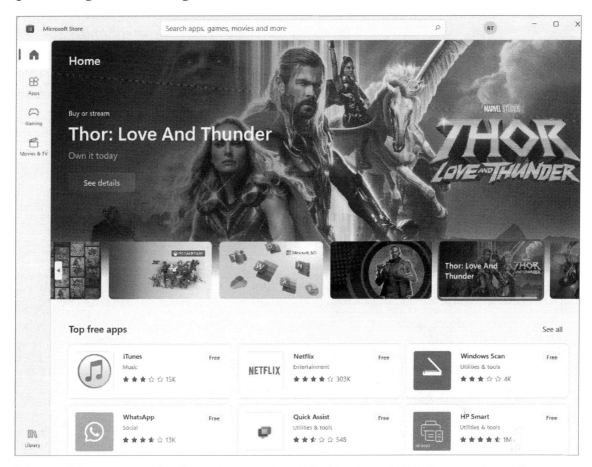

Many of the apps in the Store have a simplified look and feel that works well across Windows PCs, devices, and phones. These apps are also designed to work with touchscreens.

The Store can be opened in two ways: by clicking the Store button on the taskbar and from the All Apps list on the Start menu.

What's in the Store?

The Store has thousands of apps to choose from, and more are being added every week. While many apps are free, many others cost money, and that cost can vary. As of this writing, the Store is organized into groups (Gaming, Apps, and Movies & TV), which are further organized into dozens of categories. Since this is an online store, the organization can change at any time. If you can't find what you're looking for by clicking around, try doing a search.

⌓ HANDS-ON 10.8 Look at Apps

In this exercise, you will review some apps in the Store.

1. Click the **Store** ▣ button on the taskbar.

2. Click any category on the left side of the screen, such as **Apps** or **Gaming**.
   The Store organization and heading names can change. You are just browsing, so click any heading.

3. Scroll through the page and browse the apps.
   The stars under the names rate the app on a 1–5 scale that's based on user feedback.

4. To learn more about an app, click its icon; click the **Back** button (usually a left-facing arrow) to return to the previous page. When finished, close the Store.

Downloading Apps

Once you have found the specific apps you would like, you will click the Free or Purchase button to download. Because you are in the Store, downloading and installing of the app is all done automatically, so you can continue working on other things and be notified when the app is installed.

⌓ HANDS-ON 10.9 Download the Netflix App

In this exercise, you will download the Netflix app. Your web browser should still be open.

1. In the Chapter 10 section, click **Hands-On 10.9**.

2. Complete this exercise in the simulation.

Self-Assessment

To check your knowledge of the key concepts introduced in this chapter, complete this Self-Assessment quiz.

1.	The Search box searches items on your computer only.	**true**	**false**
2.	You can use the Search box to get help with Windows.	**true**	**false**
3.	Windows can automatically install updates.	**true**	**false**
4.	The Control Panel has been completely removed from Windows 11.	**true**	**false**
5.	Increasing the monitor's resolution makes small text sharper but also harder to read.	**true**	**false**
6.	Windows automatically checks for updates.	**true**	**false**

7. Which category will you find in Settings?

   A. System

   B. Personalization

   C. Time and Language

   D. All of the above

8. Increasing the monitor resolution _____.

   A. displays more pixels in the same amount of space on the screen

   B. makes images and text look sharper

   C. allows more images and text to fit on screen

   D. All of the above

9. Which is NOT a default power plan in Windows?

   A. Power Saver

   B. Normal

   C. Balanced

   D. High Performance

10. Which statement is NOT true about Windows Update?

   A. It checks for updates roughly once a day.

   B. Updates are installed automatically.

   C. Reboots must be done manually.

   D. It can check for updates on other installed Microsoft software.

 # Skill Builders

SKILL BUILDER 10.1 Change the Screen Resolution

In this exercise, you will change the resolution of a PC screen.

1. In the Chapter 10 section, click **Skill Builder 10.1**.

2. Complete this exercise in the simulation.
   Close your web browser when you are finished.

SKILL BUILDER 10.2 Change the Screen Background

In this exercise, you will add an image to your Desktop background.

1. Choose **Start→Settings**.

2. Click **Personalization** and then **Background**.
   This brings up the Background pane for changes to the look of the background.

3. If necessary, click the drop-down button under the Background option and choose **Picture**.

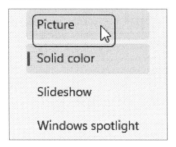

4. Click on a picture from the sample list provided.
   You can use the Browse button to find one of your own images on your PC or USB flash drive. Notice how the image selected is immediately placed on the background screen.

5. Click on the drop-down button under Background and choose **Solid Color**.

6. Select any color.
   Notice how the background immediately changes to that color.

7. Select a **Picture** or **Solid Color** to use as your background.

8. Close Settings.

SKILL BUILDER 10.3 Find and Change the Screen Saver

In this exercise, you will search settings for the screen saver controls and then enable a screen saver.

1. Choose **Start→Settings**.

2. In the Find a Setting box type: **screen saver**

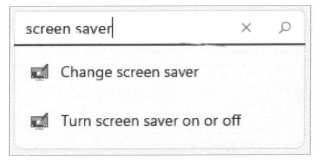

Search results will appear as you type.

3. Click **Change Screen Saver**.

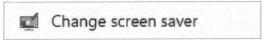

The screen saver dialog box appears. Notice that it looks different from Settings because it is from the old Control Panel.

4. The Screen Saver Settings may appear underneath the Settings screen. Click anywhere on the **Screen Saver Settings** window to make it the active program and on top.

5. From the drop-down list in the Screen Saver Settings window, choose **Mystify**.

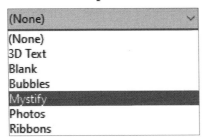

The Preview monitor at the top of the screen should show you what the screen saver looks like. The preview button can also be used to see the screen saver in full screen view.

6. Change the wait time to **5** minutes.

The screen saver will come on after 5 minutes of inactivity.

7. Look through the various screen savers, pick your favorite, and set your preferred wait time.

8. Click **OK**.

9. Close the Settings and Screen Saver Settings windows.

Self-Assessment Answer Key

Chapter 1: Getting Your First Look

	Answer	Heading or Exercise
1	true	Start Button
2	true	Icons
3	true	Icons
4	true	Mouse Motions ("Mouse Motions" table)
5	false	Shutting Down
6	false	Warning! under Passwords
7	B	Creating Your Own Passwords and "Examples of Passwords" table
8	C	Mouse Motions
9	D	Shut-Down Methods
10	D	Icons

Chapter 2: Starting and Controlling Apps

	Answer	Heading or Exercise
1	true	Touch Gestures
2	true	Multitasking
3	false	Show Desktop and Task View
4	false	Which App Is Active?
5	true	Show Desktop and Task View
6	false	Quick-Sizing Buttons and Multitasking
7	E	Quick-Sizing Buttons
8	B	Quick-Sizing Buttons ("Window Quick-Sizing Buttons" table)
9	C	Which App Is Active?
10	C	Touch Gestures ("Using Touch Gestures" table)

Chapter 3: Creating an Online Account

	Answer	Heading or Exercise
1	false	The Cloud
2	true	Account Verification
3	true	Always Logged In
4	true	Making Connections
5	true	The Cloud
6	B	Microsoft 365 for the Web, graphic under Microsoft 365 for the Web
7	D	Always Logged In

Chapter 4: Working with Apps

	Answer	Heading or Exercise
1	true	Cut, Copy, and Paste ("Cut, Copy, and Paste Commands" table)
2	true	A Portable USB Flash Drive
3	false	The Cursor and the Mouse Pointer
4	true	Where Your Work Is Located
5	true	Filenames ("Naming Files" table)
6	false	Special Keys on the Keyboard
7	A	Comment under Use Cut and Paste, step #5
8	B	Scroll Bars
9	C	Where Your Work Is Located
10	D	Save Versus Save As

Chapter 5: Using Email

	Answer	Heading or Exercise
1	true	Email Address
2	false	The Outlook Online App
3	false	Address Line
4	false	What Is Email?
5	true	Email Safety
6	true	Moving Emails
7	D	Address Line
8	D	Understanding the Threats
9	A	Moving Emails
10	D	Understanding the Threats ("Spotting a Malicious Email" table)

Chapter 6: Finding Files

	Answer	Heading or Exercise
1	false	Unplugging Safely
2	true	Searching for Files
3	true	Locating Folders
4	true	USB Flash Drives
5	true	Folders and Subfolders
6	false	Searching for Files
7	C	Navigating Your Drives and Folders
8	D	Navigating Your Drives and Folders
9	A	Behind the Screen: Common Data File Sizes
10	A	USB Flash Drives

Chapter 7: Storing Files

	Answer	Heading or Exercise
1	true	Creating Folders
2	true	How the Commands Work ("Using Cut, Copy, and Paste with Files/Folders" table)
3	false	Deleting and Restoring Folders and Files
4	false	Restoring Folders and Files
5	true	Deleting Folders and Files
6	true	OneDrive File Storage
7	D	Creating Folders
8	D	The Recycle Bin
9	D	Selecting Multiple Files ("Selecting Multiple Folders and Files" table)
10	C	OneDrive File Storage

Chapter 8: Using the Internet

	Answer	Heading or Exercise
1	false	Top-Level Domains
2	false	Routers
3	true	Hyperlinks
4	true	Favorites
5	false	Favorites Bar
6	true	Tabbed Browsing
7	C	Routers
8	D	Web Browsers

Chapter 9: Researching on the Internet

	Answer	Heading or Exercise
1	true	How Search Engines Work
2	false	The Hidden Web
3	false	Searching for Images
4	false	Searching for Images
5	true	Updating Your Software
6	false	Steps You Can Take ("Safety Steps" table)
7	D	Protection Software
8	D	Basic Search Techniques
9	B	Behind the Screen: Using Social Media Sites Safely

Chapter 10: Using Settings and Help

	Answer	Heading or Exercise
1	false	Searching Windows and the Web
2	true	Getting Help
3	true	Windows Update
4	false	Settings Versus the Control Panel
5	true	Screen Resolution Settings
6	true	Windows Update
7	D	Using Settings
8	D	Screen Resolution Settings
9	B	Additional Power Settings
10	C	Windows Update

Glossary

active   In use

aspect ratio   The relation between width and height on a computer monitor

background   The image or color covering your Desktop; also called wallpaper

bandwidth   The amount of data your Internet connection can provide

browser   A program used to access the web (*examples:* Microsoft Edge, Chrome)

cloud computing   Apps and services that run from the Internet

cloud storage   File storage on the Internet

commands   Launch a program task

cookies   Codes in webpages used to track your preferences

cursor   A blinking indicator of where text will appear on the screen when you type; *see also* insertion point

domains   Divide Internet addresses into groups with a common purpose (*examples:* .com, .net, .gov)

drag-and-drop method   A way to move screen objects in Windows

drive letter   An alphabetical designation assigned to storage devices (*examples:* C:, Removable drive F:)

favorite   A link you save in your browser

Flip   A command that allows you to switch between open apps

floppy disk   An obsolete removable disk technology

galleries   Collections of tools or options on a Ribbon

gestures   Touchscreen controls

hard drive   The permanent storage in your computer

hyperlink   A link in a web page that jumps you to another place on the web

insertion point   A blinking indicator showing where text will appear when you type on a computer; *see also* cursor

Internet service provider   *See* ISP

ISP   Internet service provider; a business that provides access to the Internet

mouse pointer   The indicator that moves on the screen in response to the movement of the mouse

networked Connected to a collection of computers and devices for the purpose of sharing information

operating system The software that manages your computer (*examples:* Windows 11, Windows 7, Windows XP, Linux, OSX)

path Shows the location of a file or folder within the organization of a drive

permanent storage A device that stores data until erased (*examples:* hard drive, USB flash drive)

pinned Items placed on the Start menu as tiles for easy access; can be organized per the user's preference

Quick Access toolbar A small toolbar containing common commands

Ribbon A program feature used to display program commands instead of using traditional menus and toolbars

router A device that enables multiple computers to connect to the Internet

search engines Specialized pages used to find information on the web (*examples:* Google.com, Ask.com)

selected Text that is highlighted and ready to be formatted or changed in some way

Settings A Windows app containing all the customization and setup controls

sleep mode Computer state in which the computer uses very little electricity and has little activity

social media sites Web pages where people and businesses are linked to discuss mutual interests

spyware A program designed to secretly gather information from your computer

subfolders Folders within a folder

Uniform Resource Locator *See* URL

URL Uniform Resource Locator; address for a resource on the Internet

viruses Small programs written to disrupt your computer

web Common name for the World Wide Web

Index

drag-and-drop method, moving files
and folders with, 179–181, 194
drives
designations of, 145–146
navigating, 150–153
viewing, 144–145, 147
Dropbox cloud storage, 59
drop-down lists (Word online app),
89–90
drop-down menus, 74
DuckDuckGo search engine, 233

E

Edge. *See* Microsoft Edge
editing text, 93–97, 116
.edu domain, 208
email
address line, 115
advance fee scam, 128–130
attachments, 118–119
Bcc and Cc, 115
composing, 116–117
deleting, 122, 137
folders, 122–124
forwarding, 120, 137–138
Gmail account, creating, 134–135
inbox, 112
interface, 112
logging in/out of, 111
moving, 124–125
online safety, 126–131
overview, 107–110
phishing, 127–128
reading, 113, 135–136
receiving, 120
replying to, 120–121
saving, 122
saving files from links, 133
sending, 113–114, 116–117,
135–136
spam, 127, 131
spoofing, 128
subject line, 115–116
email addresses, 110, 126
Enpass password manager, 6
Enter key, 92
Explorer. *See* File Explorer
external hard drives, 144

F

Facebook, 238
favorites (Microsoft Edge)
creating, 215–216, 223
enabling bar, 217–218
folders for, 218–219, 223–225
overview, 214–215
removing, 220
sorting, 219
File Explorer
common tasks in, 149
folders, 150, 169–179, 181–186
subfolders, 150, 158–159, 173
icons in, 157–159
multiple tabs in, 159–160
navigating, 150–153
overview, 149, 167–168
Recycle Bin and, 184–186
searching for files in, 161–162
sorting in, 155–157
viewing modes, 155
filenames, 79–80
files
copying, 180–181, 194
defined, 78
drive designations, 146
location, 77
moving, 176–181
naming, 79–80
on OneDrive, 189, 194–195
overview, 141–142
renaming, 171
restoring, 184–186
saving, 78–83, 98–99
searching for, 161–162
searching for content within, 165
selecting, 181–183
sending via emails, 118–119
sizes, 154
storing, 170–171
uploading to OneDrive, 195–196
Firefox, 206
firewalls, 237
Flip command, 41, 51–52
floppy disks, 146

folders
copying, 176
creating, 169–175
defined, 78
deleting, 184–186
for email, 122–124
favorites (Microsoft Edge),
218–219
locating, 150
moving, 176, 179–181
navigating, 150
OneDrive, 187–189
organizing, 177–179
overview, 157–159
renaming, 171
restoring, 184–186
selecting, 181–183
sorting, 156–157
Start menu, 22–24
subfolders, 150, 158–159, 173
formatting text, 95–97, 116
forwarding email, 120, 137–138

G

gestures, 40–41
gigabytes, 154
Gmail
account, creating, 134–135
deleting and archiving email, 137
overview, 110
sending and reading email,
135–136
Google
basic search, 228–232
basic techniques, 229
complex searches, 234–235
hidden web, 234
image searches, 235–236
improving results, 232
news searches, 244
overview, 233, 248–249
searches for copyright-safe images,
241
Google Drive cloud storage, 59
.gov domain, 208

H

hard drive (HD) storage
internal and external, 143–144
overview, 9
saving files in, 78

hardware
	hard drives, 9, 78, 143–144
	modems, 202
	mouse, 12–14
	processors, 8–9
	RAM, 9–10
	routers, 203–204
	SD card port, 11
	touchpad, 41
	types of storage media, 143–148
	USB ports, 10
hidden web, 234
high-speed Internet, 205
hyperlinks, 210

I

icons, 11–12, 157–159
images
	basic searches for, 235–236
	changing Desktop background, 263
	saving to computer, 242
	searching for copyright-safe, 241
inactive/active windows, 49
inbox (Outlook online app), 112
insertion point, 91
internal hard drives, 143
Internet
	connection types, 204–205
	country codes, 209
	dial-up, 204
	equipment needed to connect to, 202–204
	high-speed, 205
	history of, 201
	hyperlinks, 210
	icon on taskbar, 12
	ISPs, 204
	modems, 202
	navigating, 209–212
	network, 205
	overview, 199–200
	routers, 203–204
	security, 236–239
	speed of, 205
	top-level domains, 207–208
	URLs, 207–210
	web browsers, 206–207
	wireless, 205
	World Wide Web, 201–202
Internet Explorer, 206
Internet Service Providers (ISPs), 204

K

keyboard, special keys on, 91–92
keyboard shortcuts
	adding favorites, 215
	copy, 101
	cut, 101
	opening the Action Center, 44
	paste, 101
	print, 97
	select all, 93
	Start menu, showing, 18
	switching between apps, 51–52
	undo, 176
kilobytes, 154

L

LastPass, 6
LED monitor settings, 253–254
left-clicking mouse, 13
LinkedIn, 238
links. *See* hyperlinks
locking computer, 17–18
logging in/out of computer
	overview, 188
	passwords, 5–6, 15–16, 30
	startup process, 6
	steps for, 6–7, 17–18
	switching users, 16, 29
	with Microsoft account, 63–64

M

Mail.com, 110
maximizing/minimizing windows, 33–34
megabytes, 154
menu button (apps), 36
menus, 73–74
Microsoft 365 apps, 59, 68–69
Microsoft account
	always logged in, 68
	cloud-based Office apps, 59, 68–69
	connecting to Windows login, 63–64
	creating, 60–62
	online messages and pop-ups, 65
	overview, 57–58
	verifying, 60–62

Microsoft Edge
	browsing history, 221
	clearing browsing data, 243–244
	downloads, 221
	favorites, 214–223
	navigating, 209–212
	overview, 206
	printing web page, 213–214
	tabs, 211–212
Microsoft Store, 259–260
Microsoft Word. *See* Word online app
.mil domain, 208
minimizing/maximizing windows, 33–34
modems, 202
mouse
	basic actions, 13–14
	cursors, 91
	overview, 12–14
	pointers, 84, 91
	selecting text with, 93–95
	touchpad, 41
moving apps, 55
moving emails, 124–125
multitasking
	app switching, 49–52, 56
	opening multiple programs, 48–49
	overview, 48
	Show Desktop button, 52
	Task View button, 52
	usefulness of, 53

N

navigating
	drives, 150–153
	File Explorer, 150–153
	Internet, 209–212
	with keyboard shortcuts, 18, 44, 49–52
	Microsoft Edge, 209–212
	switching between apps, 41
nested folders. *See* subfolders
.net domain, 208
network connection icon (Desktop), 12
network drives, 144
network Internet, 205
news searches, 244
nonstandard app windows, 37–38
Notepad app, 43–44, 55, 56
notification area (Desktop), 12
notifications, 45–46

Word online app
Backspace key, 91
Clipboard, 100
creating copy of letter in, 106
creating letter in, 105–106
cursor and mouse pointer, 91
Delete key, 91
drop-down lists, 89–90
editing text, 93–97
Enter key, 92
formatting text, 95–97
opening, 68–69
overview, 89
printing documents, 97–99
Ribbons, 89–90
ScreenTips, 90
special keys on keyboard, 91–92
Tab key, 91
tabs, 89
typing in, 92
word-processors. *See* Word online app
work area in apps, 83–87

World Wide Web (WWW), 201–202

Y

Yahoo! Mail, 110
Yelp! 238
YouTube, 238

Z

zooming in/out, 40

Made in the USA
Columbia, SC
05 January 2025